THE DIARIES OF
A RESILIENT BLACK NURSE

An Anthology of Struggles and Achievements of black nurses in America

By Suprena Hickman
&
Expert Nurse Co-Authors:

Vianna L. Jones
Michele Derricott
Shivon Lamb Dixon
Kimberly Scott
Larnette Moore
Panza McNeill
Aron King
Cecilia McIlwain
Carolyn Burke Davis

Rina Publishing is a subsidiary of Suprena Hickman Enterprises, LLC. Our books may be purchased for educational, promotional, and business usage.

ISBN 9798716428577

Published by The Rina Publishing Co.
P.O. Box 415
Wilmington, NC 28403

First Edition

Table of Contents

Meet the Authors

Dedication

This book is dedicated to a few people who have been greatly impactful in my journey of becoming a Nurse. First, and foremost, I'm grateful to God for allowing me to serve and for blessing me with the gifts, knowledge, resilience, and loads of patience which are definitely prerequisites of nursing. I desire to continue with obedience as I know my calling to bring forth healing and restoration is a great and high honor. I don't take it lightly.

Next, I would like to dedicate this book to my mother, Annie Ravenel, who was the first unofficial Nurse I experienced. She handled all assignments with such grace, and she supported my visions- and still does. I'm also dedicating this book to my late brother, Damon Ravenel, who was my first unofficial patient, medical field educator, mentor, and cheer leader while I was in Nursing School- and in my nursing career. Also, I choose to dedicate this book to my late sister-in-law, Gail Ravenel, who recently passed this year. She was a great support as I was trying to get into college and out of college. When I graduated from Nursing School, she remained my cheerleader, but she also started the family joke calling me the "play-play Nurse". This was how she addressed me- even this year before her passing. It still makes me smile just thinking about it. Also, I dedicate this book to my husband, Brandon Hickman, for believing in me when I didn't think I could become a Nurse again. He bought me a RN pendant for my necklace before I became a RN. I wore it daily until I became a RN. I also am thankful for all of my family for their loving support during my journey of becoming a Nurse and beyond. In all that I do currently, I bring that supportive family vibe to all of my environments.

To my Nurse Educators, who helped open the doors for me and kept me motivated while in school, I thank and appreciate you. To Mrs. Julie Agles-Jankee, my nursing School advisor who was always that calm voice of reason and full of resources to guide me. To the late, Dr. Wagstaff, I appreciate the no nonsense, yet loving, approach to my nursing education at Norfolk State University. I also dedicate this book to Dr. Beverly Withers, who mentored me at her kitchen table on countless days after graduating. She trained me to have more confidence in what I've studied for years, versus studying the possible NCLEX testing questions. She always preached that if I understood the diseases down to the cellular level, then it wouldn't matter how they threw the questions at me, I would get it right. She was right and I passed the NCLEX on my first attempt.

Lastly, I dedicate this book to my aspiring black Nurses who have tirelessly attempted to enter our beloved profession unsuccessfully. I say to you, don't give up! Find a mentor who is already doing what you desire to do, sit at their feet, learn, and take massive action. You are needed and I want you to know that we support you. There are people in need of what you have, so keep pushing despite any obstacles that may arise. To my fellow black Nurses still fighting this battle of inequality, please know that freedom is within your reach. Use your voice to speak your truth. Use your heart to help spread the love in our industry, but to do this effectively, you must learn to heal your heart from your past hurts. Lastly, use your hands to facilitate healing. Let the knowledge, compassion, and joy for what you do become positively infectious. It is what I aim to do daily, and everyone mentioned above has helped- and continue to help me do and be better.

Introduction

Nursing is such an amazing, beloved, and rewarding profession. We're also known as the most trusted profession. When communicating with the doctors or medical team, Nurses are the liaisons advocating for the patients' rights. For this to occur, we must be knowledgeable about the medical profession, medications, treatments, and of course the body systems. We are the people who help to usher new life into this world. We are also the same people who are there for post-mortem care- ensuring the body is properly cared for and ensuring death certificates are properly documented.

When you go to see the doctor, you actually spend more time with the Nurse than you do with your doctor. Let's face it, Nurses have a lot of power and influence in the medical profession. If all of the Nurses decided to strike, and there were no Nursing agencies coming to bail out the hospitals and facilities, then our healthcare system would simply crumble. Nurses are a necessity, and we should indeed be celebrated. However, we tend to only highlight the joys of nursing on a national- or international platform. Everyone talks about how good nurses are, and all of the great things that nurses do.

We just don't leave much room to discuss the common issues occurring in the background beyond the nurse-patient ratios and ensuring safe practicing. You see, there are common issues that occur in our beloved profession that tends to get swept under the carpet. It's the common issues as to why there has always been a national nursing shortage. It is the common issues as to why many black nurses have struggled when it became time to be promoted. It is also the same common issues experienced once they have been promoted. It's also the common issues as to why groups of nurses from various backgrounds, throughout our country, can have conversations completely different from that of a group of black nurses in a private room. It is the common issues that actually attribute to health inequality, which can negatively affect patient care and cause distress within a community. However, there are those black nurses who have managed to persevere in the midst of these common issues, and they have managed to pave the way for those around them. There is a root to these common issues, and I've found them to include the following: Insecurities, bitterness, jealousy, hatred, envy, and racism. Well, I've found some amazing black nurses who have shared their hearts and knowledge and they are ready for a lasting and positive change for all.

So, for this project, we have united to inspire, educate, and empower the masses by simply sharing our experiences. It is our hope and desire to shine a light on the dark side of nursing, which is often unspoken, so that we may bring forth healing to our beloved profession. We can't continue to keep sweeping the issues under the rug, or tucking the common issues away in a closet, and continue to expect positive changes and growth. We can't begin to stand, united as nurses, on a shaky foundation. It's time to repair our foundation so we could rise up and bring forth positive, and lasting changes, to the medical profession. As you read their words, hear their hearts, imagine how they felt- and imagine how they may still feel. We invite you to be a part of the movement to repair our healthcare system- one nurse at a time, make a global impact, and help change healthcare for the betterment of our patients. Let's start speaking up against inequality. Let's stifle the voices of the oppressors. Let us create more safe spaces to allow free speech- without fear of retaliation. Let's use our voices, positions, and platforms to bring forth positive changes. We can do this!

Suprena Hickman, Your Escape Coach

Forward

During my career as a surgeon, I have learned a lot about wounds. The human body is incredibly resilient and able to recover from all kinds of wounds, as long as proper healing conditions are met. This always leaves a scar of some sort, but the scars represent reinvigorated tissue, which is often as strong as before, and is commonly highly functional. Yet inevitably healing conditions are not met in all cases, and sometimes the wound remains unhealed at the risk of great peril to the patient. Severe infection, limb loss, and death all become potential outcomes of non-healing wounds. And so, it is with racism in American health care. A great unhealed wound remains, as evidenced by obvious outcome disparities. This wound imperils many, and in fact the low overall health of our nation reflects just how dangerous our situation has become. Life expectancy is dropping, and the people of the United States find our health ranking incredibly low among developed nations, despite exorbitant levels of spending.

So, what would a well-healed scar of wounded health look like in our country? It would certainly enable a much higher rank among developed nations, along with a reduced-price tag for people. Bankruptcy due to a health care expenditure would not occur. Patients would get the safe, high reliability care they expect, and outcomes would be equitable because all people would have opportunities to reach their highest levels of health. Disease prevention and health maintenance would reign supreme. There would be no disparities, and although people would require less hospital-based care because of generally improved health, when hospitalization was required the patient experience would be remarkable no matter the demographic of the patient. The needs of the patients would come first, and the focus would be upon the person with the illness, not on the disease itself as is so often the case today.

The real question becomes how we get there. At a time when we seem to be at an all- time low of interpersonal understanding, in environments that are often segregated along racial lines, creating an atmosphere of inclusion seems particularly daunting. An environment so complex will require a number of interventions to create the opening for people to step into, but when that opening occurs people must be ready to step into the space. It is just such a step that organizations such as Sankofa Training & Wellness Institute are preparing people to take. Quite simply, the equity gap in the professional workforce must be filled first, in order to optimize the opportunity to close the equity gaps in care. Numerous studies now confirm that patient experience, patient satisfaction, and patient outcomes are positively impacted when there is racial concordance between patient and provider, yet we find our health care workforce profoundly discordant with the populations we serve. We are doomed to repeatedly create poor health outcomes until we repair this discordance and cultivate a workforce that looks like the population. And this is when things begin to come together, because the outcome of addressing the needs of a population being least well served always carries over to a result that all population outcomes are improved by any intervention on the population with greater challenges.

Healing the wounds of the African American health care workforce is henceforth a necessary step to creating acceptable health outcomes for all populations. This wound, the result of recurrent elimination of training and advancement opportunities, is longstanding but healing is possible. There are many pathways through which to accomplish this healing, all of which begin with new opportunities consistent with those extended to other demographic groups throughout history. For so long, policies, processes and procedures have prevented minorities of all kinds, but particularly African Americans, from advancing to high level health careers in any discipline. This can be tracked across every "white coat" career in health care, and it is completely correctable. I am encouraged to see more open dialogue beginning to address these opportunity factors for black health care professionals, but dialogue alone will not suffice. We know we are facing a massive workforce shortage, especially in the wake of the COVID-19 global pandemic. This will provide new opportunities to expand the workforce with people who represent the populations who have for too long gone unrepresented, and as a benefit the quality of our health care outcomes for all populations will increase. Of course, there are those who will wish to hang on a little longer, to look longingly backward to the past while the breathtaking pace of change accelerates beyond them. But that will not be the people reading this book. No, you are committed to understanding a little more, to making the courageous leaps into the health care equity paradigm of the future. It's an exciting time, and I am glad we are all on this journey, together!

Dr. Philip Brown

Dr. Philip Brown, Jr.

MD, FACS

L abeled as a "dent-maker" by his mentors and coaches, Dr. Philip Brown is known for disrupting organizations and systems. As a statewide leader guiding the vision and direction of healthcare through numerous roles with NC Medical Society, Brown influenced the organization to increase diversity in its leadership and include health equity as a guiding principle. Additionally, he established the department of Health Equity & Human Experience as one of many areas under his oversight as Executive Vice President and Chief Physician Executive with New Hanover Regional Medical Center.

Dr. Brown was recently appointed Chief Community Impact Officer for Novant Health where he assumed responsibility for developing strategy for provider workforce equity and public health policy. He will also lead efforts in Social Responsibility, Community Wellness, Community Benefit, and Community Engagement and Partnerships.

Dr. Brown received his MD from the Brody School of Medicine at East Carolina University in 1995 and a BA in Physical Education from UNC Wilmington in 1988 where he graduated Cum Laude. He's been licensed by the North Carolina Medical Board since 1998 and certified by the American Board of Surgery both in general and vascular surgery. Brown completed his general surgery residency at the Brody School of Medicine in 2001 and was a Fellow in Vascular Surgery with Johns Hopkins Hospital in 2001-2002. His scope of practice included two years in academic surgery followed by twelve years in private practice before taking on full-time health care executive roles in 2016.

Suprena Hickman

Suprena Hickman

RN, BSN, MBA

Suprena Hickman is a registered nurse of 20 plus years- who now, as a Nurse Entrepreneur, chooses to use her stethoscope differently. The community of which she serves is her hospital and/or clinic. Suprena is the Co-Founder and Executive Director of Better is Possible CDC, Inc.- which is a 501C3 nonprofit organization providing personal development, mentoring, wellness, & scholarship support to her community with the assistance of her husband and executive board. She has created and managed programs such as Escape 2 Sisterhood weekend retreats, Girls Rocking in the South (GRITS), and Port City Rip the Runway all for over a decade. As a social entrepreneur, she uses her gifts of creativity, healing, and organization, to bring forth positive changes in her community and beyond. She is the CEO, or Chief Escape Officer, of Suprena Hickman Enterprises, LLC (SHE)- which includes Escapes in A Box, LLC; Sankofa Training & Wellness Institute, LLC; Your Escape Coach, LLC; and Sweet Escapes by Suprena. SHE offers a unique approach to healing- even with her baked goodies! Suprena's mission with SHE is to help women heal. Her mission with Sankofa Training & Wellness Institute is to educate, empower, and bring more black talent into the medical profession. Suprena regularly empowers the lives of women and teen girls through her coaching, adult and youth mentorship, workshops, wellness retreats, and live events.

For nearly a decade of her career, Suprena has traveled within the country providing direct support to hospitals, clinics, and community organizations. Suprena understands the impact self-sacrifice can have on one's personal health by placing the needs of others before their own. As Suprena has learned to heal herself, she has continued to share her process of healing- physically, mentally, and spiritually. Suprena is a proud graduate of Norfolk State University- where she received her Bachelor of Science degree in Nursing, and she also received her Master of Business Administration from the University of Phoenix. Suprena is also a Certified Integrative Health Coach- trained by Duke Integrative Medicine. Suprena is a member of American Nurses Association, National Nurses in Business Association, The American Holistic Nurses Association, North Carolina Nurses Association, National Black Nurses Association, & International Coach Federation. She currently serves on the Board of Directors for the YWCA Lower Cape Fear and also NSEA Swim Foundation. She is currently married with one child and she is a caregiver/care manager for her mom out of state. She has great passion for caregivers and other high-achieving women.

Purpose Over Problems

My Nursing Inspiration

I was a young black woman- eager to learn, very inquisitive, and extremely flexible entering the medical field- by any means necessary. I was likely inspired by my mother and my brother- of whom was diagnosed with renal disease before he became a year old. My mom was his caregiver as she also cared for everyone else in our family when needed- which was often. She was the first nurse of whom I've ever been exposed to because my brother grew up having frequent hospitalizations due to treatments and surgical procedures. Quite often, she administered his medications, cleansed his wounds, comforted him, made sure he got into dialysis treatments, and she even gave him one of her kidneys.

Then, there was my brother who was the fully informed patient verbalizing his medical regimen- including medications and medical teams. He even had knowledge of his renal functions, like his creatine, BUN, and blood pressure readings. He was aware of it all. He knew his stuff and he asked a lot of questions. Both my mom and brother were very close because of his illness- and she was his caregiver and nurse. They both continued to push through, despite any hardships that existed with caring for him. You see, I had older siblings, but my brother and I were the last two in the home- and my mom raised us by herself. Both my mom and my brother were resilient.

I was born and raised in beautiful and historic downtown Charleston, South Carolina. I was an inner-city girl and an at-risk youth who could've fallen by way of the streets. In middle school, it was a normal sight to see teens as parents or selling drugs. Honestly,

I didn't know that I was lacking anything- nor do I feel I was lacking anything as a child. My mom provided me and my brother everything. She worked hard daily at a local college as a custodian. However, I also recall accompanying her to clean large houses along the Battery and she was masterful at making it all look easy. Our lights were always on. Our water was always on. I always had clothing- even if it were "hand-me-downs". We all did. She also kept me exposed to many things. Every time she heard of some afterschool or summer program, then you better believe that I was in it. Being raised in the house, we often had a house full, because my mom always made room for my nieces and nephews. She even made room for temporarily displaced family due to hurricanes.

So basically, if anybody she considered family, needed a place to stay, they had a place to stay. My resilient mom was able to manage all of this stuff, and be that super woman, while taking care of a chronically ill child with multiple hospitalization, surgeries, and clinic visits. Oh, and she didn't miss a beat either. They were both informed and educated as a caregiver and a patient. My mom often told me that a black nurse pulled her to the side early on and stressed the importance of her knowing what was going on with her child's care. This clearly stuck with her- as she was an excellent caregiver for us all. My brother wasn't promised to live and see one year, but he actually lived a very purposely life and didn't pass away until age forty-two. I attribute this to the care and attentiveness of my mom being an amazing caregiver, my brother being an outstanding patient, and their top-notch medical team over at Medical University of South Carolina. They were just the epitome of resilience. So, I believe that's why I became a nurse. It was natural to want to care for other people.

I was also babysitting my nieces and nephews a lot to help out my siblings. As their babysitter, I provided structure, reviewed homework if needed, read books, prepared meals, took administered medications and helped to clean those "boo-boos" when needed. I was able to create a classroom for learning- which involved the arts, right there in my own home. It was fun! So, basically, I played their teacher and nurse. I became really good at managing and multitasking. Meantime, amongst all of this, my mom was active in her church and Ushers Council, therefore, she was always creating live events in the church to help raise funds for the church. I believe this kept her mind from focusing on the heavy assignment that she had at home with raising my brother. She loved all of her kids- and still does, so she didn't look at it as a burden. I believe she was honored to have the opportunity to simply do what she could to help. However, in all that she would do, there had to be order! Annie didn't play- and she still doesn't. Her programs would have some order, a theme, and start on time. If you read my bio, then I think you would understand where I get it all from. I get it from my momma! So, yes, all of this went down in my home growing up- and I wouldn't trade a thing because it has molded me into the resilient Nurse Boss I am today.

Homie the Clown

I will never forget having the science teacher in high school, who was always making fun of the kids who did not come out to be superior in his class, I called him "Homie the Clown", which was a 1990's character on a night sketch comedy show called, "In Living Color". He was a tall, black male with a bald head in the middle and hair on the sides and back. He was a clown in my eyes. He played around with some kids and then there were others (most of them) whom he literally made fun of and terrorized in class. I seriously doubt he liked his job. I feel he was placed there and used what he had to get where he wanted in the meantime. He always referenced his former job with the police department in New York. This was something that he always loved, but somehow, he ended up teaching school down South. It seemed like he got a kick out of just making fun of the kids. I did not feel as if he loved helping us. He would give us grades as low as a five on a test or an assignment, and he would just make fun of it and stand in front of the class and laugh like crazy. He didn't make science fun and he would literally have outbursts where he would throw the chairs or desk over in the classroom while fussing at a kid. Oh, the drama and the intimidation he would bring. He was a bully and was quick to call someone dumb or stupid.

One day, he told me that I was too dumb to be a nurse. He said this in front of the class. This was a day he felt like picking on more kids after another test where the majority of his class failed. He was asking everyone what we wanted to do when we graduated. This was my senior year, and I was taking his Physics class from Hell. He told me I needed to pass his class if I wanted to be a nurse, but then he said, "you're too stupid to be a nurse". He then continued and said, "you're dumb and nurses gotta be smart". I'll never forget that because in that moment, when he said that, I was hurt. Of course, some kids just looked and didn't say anything, and then some would laugh. He just got a kick out of it because he was an attention seeker, very loud and boisterous, but never seeming compassionate to me at all. I was stuck with him for three years as a science teacher and I was thinking, good God, they couldn't find anybody else to teach science at the school. He came from New York to teach at a poor, predominantly black school. I ended up getting him for biology, chemistry, and physics. He was just horrible and when we complained to other teachers, and the principal, nothing really happened. I'm thinking that they couldn't replace him, so we were stuck with him. I later found out that he lied to me. Physics was not a prerequisite for Nursing school- and it still isn't. So, I withdrew from his class after the first semester. He was just horrible. I also recall telling my mom about him and my mother tried to schedule an appointment with him at parent teacher conference. My mom took off from work (this was HUGE growing up in a black family and a single parent home). She was a single mom trying to make it, and she took off from work and came to the school to advocate for me. He was nowhere to be found. Nobody knew where he had disappeared. He intentionally did not want to meet with my momma. He just preferred to be a bully. The damaging part was the fact that the principal never checked him on that behavior. There didn't seem to be any accountability whatsoever. The beauty of sharing this memory is that I stayed the course, graduated, went to college, and became a Nurse. I met my husband in college, who eventually graduated and became a teacher in the Charleston area- a few miles away from where I went to high school. He landed a job teaching at a school in a rural area where Homie the Clown, of all people, was the Assistant Principal. This school was another predominantly black school. So, basically, after all of his bullying mess, he got promoted! That's the mouth wide open part for me, but the beauty of it is that he literally ran into me one day after school when I was meeting my husband (boyfriend at that time). He saw me in my Nursing uniform with my badge on, because I came there straight from work. We were both shocked to see each other. But do you know what he had the nerve to say? He called my name and said, "I knew you would become a nurse." I remember giving a blank stare, shook my head, rolled my eyes, and I kept walking. I never said anything to him. Although, I do wish that I had said something like: Hey Homie the Clown! I'm a Travel Nurse now, and I probably make more than you do annually, and I never had to take physics either. I'm cracking up as I write this, but those were real feelings. I just didn't have the guts to say it because I was still raised to respect my elders. So, although I didn't say anything to him, I believe that having him simply see me in my uniform with my badge on was enough.

Clowned of Confidence

It was a constant battle for me to be great. It was hard for me to simply show up and do what I was trained to do- and be the best nurse that I could be. It was a constant battle for me to always try and learn new things every day because I kept hearing his voice in the back of my head. Homie the Clown lived in my head rent free for years after I no longer was being taught by him. I heard a voice and felt my thoughts telling me that I was too dumb to be a nurse. I also didn't see many Nurses who looked like me, so therefore, I started believing what I was hearing and feeling. I heard that you have to be smart to be a Nurse. I had somehow convinced myself that I wasn't smart. I graduated with a college prep track and had some college credits under my belt prior to entering college, yet I chose to believe the voice of the enemy telling me that I was too dumb to be a Nurse. My confidence was shaken when it was time for me to enter my Nursing program. I struggled my first year with the basics on paper. However, I always did amazing in clinicals. I engaged in the classes and answered questions when called upon, but I still didn't believe in me enough. Therefore, I wasn't successful in my first year of my Nursing program. I made a C- in Fundamentals of Nursing. There was no repeating the testing. There also was no such as making a C in the Nursing program- let alone making a C-. It was an automatic dismissal. I was devastated and confused. How could I have failed this course. It covered just the basics of Nursing like bathing, grooming, bed making, medical terminology, and more. It was basically a Nurse Aide training level course. These were the things that I actually learned at home with my mom and my brother. I just didn't have the formal words and theory lessons from my mom and brother. So, how dare I not be successful? It is all about confidence. That's really it. I studied hard. I was in the study groups. I stopped all extracurricular activities. I showed up to where I needed to be. However, I was still bearing the weight of a broken little boy, trapped in a grown man's body, disguised as my Science Teacher- and he was a clown and a bully living rent free in my head.

Thank God I had and amazing Nurse Advisor to give me sound advice regarding how to continue pursuing Nursing without changing my major. After realizing that I needed to repeat the course, and all that was involved in repeating it, I was so down and discouraged. I naturally went to speak with one of my nursing instructors who looked like me, and she spent nearly an hour trying to convince me to change my major. You would've thought I was failing miserably in school- and I wasn't. However, she tried to push me to the Social Work department so I could still graduate on time. I insisted that I wanted to be a Nurse. This older black woman, whom could've been my mother, looked at me and said that's your only option. You see, in order for me to repeat the course, I would've had to wait for the class to be available again in the Fall, then register to "audit" the course. This means, I would take the course and not get a grade, but I would get a pass or fail for attending or not. Then, upon completing the audit of the course, I would then be eligible to re-apply for the program and enter in the Fall- not the Spring. So, that would've been an entire year passing by with me continuing to wait- and there wasn't a guarantee that I would've been accepted.

My confidence decreased even more. Furthermore, I couldn't tell my mom because I was embarrassed and feared she was gonna kill me. You see, if you audit a course, then financial aid doesn't cover courses without credits. Also, it didn't even count for my hours. I couldn't advance to the next courses and I didn't have anything else I could take in school. That damn Homie the Clown resurfaced again telling me of how I was too dumb to be a Nurse. I just felt hopeless until I spoke with my Nursing Advisor, a young white woman who always spoke so soft and passionate. She loved her job of helping us student nurses. I told her of my concerns and cried trying to figure it all out on my own. She calmly told me of another option. I was all ears. The plan was to go to a neighboring institution and enroll in the Licensed Practical Nurse (LPN) program. It was only a year in length. I was to graduate and gain work experience while I await re-entry in the Nursing program at my college. Listen! That was the BEST solution ever! It worked. She didn't try to get me to change my major. She listened to my problem and she provided advise for my situation. I applied and got accepted to start in the Fall. She suggested that I look at a program at the local hospital to stay on top of my clinical skills called, "Nurse Care Partner". It was a combination of a CNA and LPN combined. I did everything the LPNs did except administer medications. I did that training in the Summer, while I awaited the school year to begin. All of a sudden, I realized I was no longer hearing Homie the Clown's voice anymore. I was also working fulltime in a Level 1 Trauma Hospital beside Nurses, Doctors, and more- only a couple of months after failing Nursing Fundamentals. The things I didn't pass was what I was literally doing daily. I was taking care of patients from all walks of life. I also realized that the more knowledge and skills I learned, the more confident I became.

By the time I entered the LPN program in the Fall, I was balancing working a fulltime job and being in the program fulltime. However, this time around, I barely focused on clinicals because it was my top strength. I was able to focus more on the theory and rationale as to why certain clinical actions were to be taken. That made me become a better Nursing Care partner- or Nurse Tech. I completed the program successfully and passed the State Board examination (NCLEX) on the first attempt. All of this occurred within a little over a year. I completely changed the trajectory of my Nursing career- and I owe it all to God for sending my Angel to guide me in the right direction. I worked for a bit to get more nursing experience, then I returned to my college and immediately got accepted into the program by way of another special one-year program. It was a Second-Degree program that only lasted a year. I was totally winning and earning a salary at the same time. Confidence and experience were key but mentoring by the right person actually made a difference.

Mammy and Me

After enjoying nearly, a decade of a Travel Nursing career, with acute care experiences ranging from Medical/Surgical, to Cardiac Intensive Care Units- with an occasional Emergency Room fix, I decided to try something new. I began working for a Federal Agency. I had this spastic, Nurse Manager who was very masterful at "looking busy". She walked, and oftentimes, ran up and down the hallways looking as if she is conquering emergent episodes back-to-back daily. She just loved to "pick my brain" on a daily basis. It got to a point where I was literally doing her work for her. I helped to set up the new clinic, so it was like having a new house. I knew everything about anything that was going on in the building regarding building maintenance on to clinical management. I even assigned teams and assisted with putting out "fires" in the clinic regarding patients and staff. I also was able to look at resumes to advise her of whom to hire. I assisted with weekly reports and even picked out food for the staff's luncheons. I also was the person vetted to orient new Nurses coming on board. I shared these responsibilities with another RN buddy I worked with at that time. I didn't realize everything I was doing until I was venting to another co-worker at a different location, and she told me to stick to my job duties only. The more we did for this manager, the more she became dependent upon us to keep doing for her. My Nurse buddy and I would arrive at least an hour early and we would stay there pretty late trying to get work done that we couldn't get done during the day because we were too busy doing her work. It was so bad that whenever there were formal inspections, my nurse buddy and I did it and gave the tours. However, when it was time to give awards and honors, we were often forgotten about. There were no special recognitions for the work we've been putting in.

One day, I decided that I would no longer tolerate the disrespect. She pretended as if she was doing all of the work by herself. She would study the works that we did and come back to ask questions for clarification. I finally listened at her door one day, as her office was next to mine, and I heard her taking credit for the works we did. I spoke to her about it, and she said she has to "justify her job". So, she basically admitted what she had been doing to me, but was not going to change it; so, I changed it. I stopped offering the assistance. She noticed the withdrawal and became snappy and divisive with me. The staff started treating me differently as well. She would start going in and out of the clinics excessively huddling inappropriately like a broken little girl, trapped in a grown woman's body. She acted out because she couldn't have her way. She then said to me, as she kneeled down, in a final plea for my help, "Suprena, you remind me of my mammy, and I miss her so much. I hope we could get closer like we used to be." I looked at her and said, "I know you couldn't possibly believe that this is flattery?" I then logged off of the computer and walked away to calm down. My Nurse buddy overheard the conversation, and we were both offended.

You see, this Nurse Manager was a white woman, with blonde hair, who was small in frame, and rather incompetent for the position of which she was hired. These are often the types of people who land these positions first. You see, my Nurse Buddy and I both applied for her position and we didn't get it. Instead, we both became staff Nurses for the clinic and eventually shared roles managing the clinic. We were competent but rejected. Could it have been the color of our skin? Maybe it was the fat on our backs. We were "two chocolate bunnies" with meat on our bones, who could run circles around our colleagues and Nurse Manager with regard to the clinic; hence, the Mammy syndrome she had. The Mammies back in the days typically were the big, black women who could run the homes of Massa and his family. The Mammies even breast-fed their boss's white babies. So, with all that I did alone for her, of course she would act out because I stopped being her Mammy- which I never knew I was doing.

We were in an oppressed and toxic environment expecting great changes positively. Furthermore, I was upset with myself for not practicing boundaries with my manager. She could only do to me what I allowed. I cared about the clinic and my patients, but I also sought out validation from my boss and her bosses. I never got that from them, however, the CEO of the organization was quite fond of my work. She mentioned me in their big morning meetings quite a few times and she often would stop by and give me encouragement, whenever she was visiting the clinic, about "being a pioneer". I never quite understood what she meant probably because I was so filled with hurt and anger with my environment. However, I definitely understand it now. My manager wanted me all to herself so that she could look good. I was easier to control and manipulate at that time as opposed to my Nurse buddy, who was a retired Naval Commander- and older. We made reports, but nothing positive came of it. The more I reported, the worse my job actually became. Eventually, this manager was given an opportunity to change positions- by force. Yep, upper management finally deemed her incompetent for the position after a couple of years or so in that position- after so much damage was done. In the meantime, who do you think was selected to help temporarily manage the clinic while we await a new Nurse manager? You got it. Me! A different manager covering the facility appointed me as the "go-to" person in charge. So, here I go with submitting weekly reports again and so much more. It was more hectic because my Nurse manager was now working under me and beside me. Oh, the chaos she caused. Oh, the divisiveness she caused. Oh, the drama she kept coming. You know what was worse? I was now deemed public enemy number one because the word on the street was that I caused her to lose her job. No one person has such power in a federal system. I was thinking, well damn, I just can't be great.

However, greatness has always been within me. I simply needed to heal from all of the hurts that constantly presented itself my way. The hurts, pain, and stressors caused excessive inflammation in my body. I was dealing with massive uterine fibroid tumors in my body which doubled in size within a year. I was hemorrhaging nearly daily- and I had tracked it to match my stress level. So, on days and weeks where my stress level was extremely high, then the more I bled. I was placed on so many medications as a result of it to control the bleeding and other side effects of it. It got to the point where I was taking a vinyl lunch bag size filled with medications every day and I was in some doctor's clinic nearly every week. Do you know that I remained in this toxic environment for a few years? My confidence was "shook", I referred to the workplace as "the plantation", and to top it all off, the new Nurse Manager (another short, white woman with blonde hair who flirted with all of the doctors) would frequently huddle behind closed doors with the former Nurse Manager- who once told me that I reminded her of her Mammy. This new Nurse Manager started treating me the same as the former Nurse Manager who was forced to step down and work alongside and under us. I say "under" because she wasn't even allowed to be the Charge Nurse. That's how incompetent she was. Yet, she was allowed to take up space and cause destruction in the workplace because it was simply the federal system's rules that allowed her to remain. It's called job security.

So, I finally left after I declared no more of the toxicities. I was willing to take a pay cut for peace. I remember surrendering to God and declaring peace over my life. I felt I was dying inside. I needed to escape the cycle of toxicities in that system- as it was destroying everything in me. I submitted my resignation with only a two-week notice. There is something amazing about surrendering to God. You see, I submitted my resignation on a Monday and literally only had to work Tuesday, Wednesday, and a half of a day on Thursday- because I had a dental appointment scheduled. Our clinic was closed on Fridays. The following week, I had a scheduled leave of absence that was already in the books nearly two months prior. The next day was a Tuesday before the Fourth of July, and I needed to get to the main facility- which required travel out of town. There was a specific check-out process for employees exiting the system. However, because it was a holiday week, everything shifted, and it moved my final day of exiting up by a couple of days. I never had to re-enter my toxic work environment as I knew it. I went early in the morning and cleared out my office and turned in my keys to the main facility. Everything happened so fast and smooth. I didn't have another job lined up, but I was excited about the peace I had. I also was confident in the Lord to lead me down the path of righteousness. I knew that whatever I was to do next would be way better than the previous years of Hell I faced under the system that fully supported toxicities like a white woman calling and treating her black employee like her Mammy. Oh, I was finally free. It was at this point where I decided to start using my stethoscope differently and I walked fully into entrepreneurship. My sole focus was on healing.

KKK versus Prena

There was a time when I was working in a local acute care facility in the Coronary Care Unit. There were only two black nurses working in this unit. This particular night, I was the only black nurse working and of course I was given the assignment with only one patient so that I could have the admission. We were otherwise full and had no other beds available. This didn't bother me because I always liked to stay busy. It made the night go by faster. Well, I received word that a new admission was coming in and I took the report from the Nurse in the Emergency Room. The patient arrived having just experienced a massive heart attack. He was alert and responsive and "very sweet". I received the remaining report and he arrived shortly afterwards. It was customary to have "all hands-on deck" when a new patient arrives so the Nurse would have assistance getting the patient settled. As I entered the room, I naturally took the lead role. I introduced myself to him with a smile and began getting him transferred from the stretcher to the bed. I started changing his telemetry monitoring leads, which monitors his heart, so that I could see what his heart rhythm and other stats were running. As soon as I touched him, he swatted at me and started threatening me. He dared me to touch him again. I assumed he was confused possibly due to oxygen deprivation. Nope. It was when he started referring to me as a "nigger" is when I realized what was going on.

I continued to attempt to calm him down while we were trying to get him settled in the room. I needed to restart his IV and so much to prepare him for a procedure. He cussed at me, spat at me, kicked at me, threatened me, and every single colleague of mine all stood around in the room watching. This patient told me he was going to call his boys to come see about me if I touched him one more time. I wanted clarification on who his boys were, and he said the Klan. I then asked him was a member. He said, "you damn right I am". He said that with such confidence. I remember saying that I thought they didn't openly speak about their involvement in the Klan. He told me where his people were located, and they could get rid of me with a quickness. I, then continued to work as I was speaking to him- hoping he would calm down, but he simply refused to have me as his Nurse.

He was allowed to continue with the insults and combativeness toward me, but when I spoke up to defend myself, I was silenced by my Charge Nurse, who was a white male. He said, "that's enough Suprena." You see, all of my colleagues were all white women and men, and no one came to my defense at all. I will never forget that feeling of hurt I felt as I continued to push through trying to take care of this patient. Here I am, this plus-sized chocolate beauty, feeling confident with my amazing clinical skills and medical knowledge, working in a specialized Intensive Care Unit, while sporting my afro, looking neat and clean, just somehow got diminished to just a damn nigger. I'm from the south, so a white male or female calling me a nigger sadly doesn't bother me too much. I know who I am and who I am not.

It was the lack of support from my colleagues of whom I thought would speak up, and they didn't! They all left the room and huddled in groups of 2-3. You see, no one wanted the new admission because it is a lot of work. Eventually, the Charge Nurse reassigned me, and I traded patients with another Nurse. Absolutely NO ONE spoke of it again. It was as if it never happened. No one said I'm sorry you had to deal with that Suprena. It was the most humiliating and irritating thing I've experienced at that time. It was enough to let me know that it was time to go. If this was allowed, then I assumed my license would be in jeopardy if I stayed. I wanted to simply do my job without the artifacts in the way. I needed to get to a location that had much more diversity because clearly these people were not accustomed to seeing many black nurses- especially in a specialized unit. We are normally placed heavily in the Medical/Surgical units and long-term care units. So, my presence was shocking for not only the staff members, but also for my lovely Klansman.

Wisdom

What I know now, I wish I understood in all of those moments I've shared. You can't love and respect anyone unless you start loving and respecting yourself first. The problem is that we lack true self-care. When we begin caring for ourselves, then we learn to look within our heart and soul and desire to cleanse deeply. As you clean your heart, mind, and soul, then you move differently. Your behaviors will change. You will forgive more easily. You will seek understanding. You will lack insecurities. You will ditch the "broken little boy/girl trapped in a grown man/woman's body" syndrome. Your behaviors will naturally be infectious and spread to your colleagues, your patients, and even your family members. Toxic behaviors exist because of a lack of self-care. It's that deep spiritual connection that is missing for so many. It causes them to not be aware of who they are and what their purpose is in life. We are living amongst so many who are wandering around lost and purposeless. This is why their fruits are rotten. We recognize them by the fruits they bear (Mathew 7:20). I'm one hundred percent clearer on my purpose in life today than I was during those earlier times in my career. I have no regrets. I needed to experience it all in order to truly appreciate the peace and clarity that I now possess. Now that I have peace, I protect it. Purposeful living keeps me focused, grateful, and peaceful. I pray the same for you.

Shivon Lamb-Dixon

Shivon Lamb-Dixon

MSN, RN, RN-BC

Shivon Lamb-Dixon has been a registered nurse for a total of twelve years this year. She received her associate degree in nursing from Cape Fear Community College in 2009. She went on to complete her Bachelor's in Nursing in 2014 at Kaplan University and became a member of Sigma Theta Tau. In 2018, she graduated from Purdue University Global with honors with a Master's degree in Nurse Education. Shivon became board certified in nurse case management in 2018 as well. Shivon is now attending Purdue University Global for a post-graduate certificate to become a Family Nurse Practitioner. All of this has been achieved while being a single parent to three beautiful girls which include twins that are seventeen and an adorable eight-year-old. Shivon is very passionate about the health and well-being of the minorities in her community that may or may not have access to healthcare. Shivon hopes to share her story to inspire others to never stop reaching for their dreams and also to help bring change to her profession and community.

Rising Through Adversity

Being a nurse in America is a very rewarding and challenging career. When you add being a minority to the mix, it can make for a very interesting and even more challenging career. In life, we all go through obstacles, trials, and tribulations. It is not about what you have been through, it is about how you push through, rise forward, and move past it. It is about following your dreams and aspirations and not letting anything, or anyone stops you or hold you back from it. From the time when I was a little girl, I always knew I wanted to be in the medical field. I have had personal challenges, racial inequalities, and career challenges try to get in the way of me succeeding and fulfilling my dream. In this diary, you will read about the obstacles, racial inequalities, and the challenges of the career itself that has made me the person I am today. I am a resilient black nurse.

Personal Obstacles

I was raised an only child by my mother. My father was not in my life due to unforeseen circumstances. I will never forget when I was in middle school, a teacher told me that the odds were against me. I did not know at the time what she meant, so I asked what do you mean? She said "Your socioeconomic status, your race, and the fact that you do not have a father in your life mean that the odds are against you and you are less likely to succeed in life and go to college and have a career. I remember coming home and telling my mother about this. My mother immediately spoke positivity in my life. This has and will always stick with me. Every trial and tribulation I have gone through in my life reminded me of those words spoken to me by my middle school teacher. Regardless, I kept telling myself I had to do better and beat the odds.

When I was in high school, I decided that I wanted to be a doctor. Not just any doctor, a neonatologist. A neonatologist is a doctor who specializes in the care of newborn children. Remember this, it will be important later. Unfortunately, I experienced my first death of someone I knew while I was in high school. At that time, it was so much hurt and fear in my heart, I decided I did not have what it takes to be a doctor. I feared a patient dying and the guilt hurt, and fear I may feel. I was afraid of having to tell a mother and father their child died. It was at that moment that I decided that I needed a different career choice. I decided I would go to college to be a clinical laboratory scientist. I have always been intrigued by diseases and I always thought it would be cool if I could find a cure for cancer or AIDS. When I graduated high school, I went to college to be a clinical laboratory scientist. Unfortunately, two years into the program, the college dropped the program. It was no longer offered. I was at a crossroads at that point and did not know what to do. I had previously taken many psychology courses so the easiest thing to do at the time was to change my major to psychology. I knew that was not where my heart was, however, I did not want to be in college longer than I would have been. Now that I am much older and wiser, I know things like this happen when we try to solve problems or issues on our own instead of praying, fasting, and looking to God for answers. He is the ultimate problem solver. I should have never changed from my dream to be a doctor because of my fears. For the Bible says in 2 Timothy 1:7 that For God hath not given us the spirit of fear, but of power, and love, and of a sound mind.

While I was attending college after the program was dropped and I was forced to change my major to one I did not want because I already had plenty of classes towards that major and it would not prolong my years in college, I found out I was pregnant. Not only was I pregnant, but I was pregnant with twin girls. While trying to manage college and pregnancy, I went into preterm labor. That required me to be hospitalized for the remainder of my pregnancy. I ended up in the hospital for five weeks on bed rest with one wheelchair ride a week. On Fridays, my mom would wheel me downstairs and take me outside for fresh air. It was one of the scariest times of my life. My twin girls ended up being born ten weeks early. They spent two months a total of eight weeks in the neonatal intensive care unit. I was a young twenty-three years old and I was scared to death. I had the privilege of having some awesome nurses. They were so patient with me and they were so good to my girls. They took pictures of them when I could not be there. I went every four hours during "touch time" to see them. I remember thinking God, why did this have to happen to me. Well….thinking back when I was in high school, I wanted to be a neonatologist to care for premature babies. Now I have two premature babies on my own to care for. At that instant when I had that revelation, I knew that I had to go to school to be a nurse. Those nurses had such a positive impact on my life that I wanted to be that person for someone else that was scared and did not know what to do or how to process what was happening. I truly believe that experience was God's way of showing me what my calling and my career path should be.

I decided to enroll in nursing school when the twins were a year old. I was married and working a full-time job forty hours per week. I started with the pre-requisite courses first. I took one to two classes here and there. During this time of my life, I was twenty-four years old and my husband was twenty-three years old. We were young and new parents of two little girls. We started having problems in our marriage that I won't go into here. I planned to get all my pre-requisite courses done before applying to the nursing program. Due to the problems, I was facing, I decided to go ahead and apply. I did not get in. I was crushed and did not know what to do. My thought was God, this is your plan for my life, why is it not working out? Well…things got worse in my marriage and I became a single mother when the twins had just turned three years old. I knew I needed to finish school, and have an actual career so that I could take care of them. I had finished all my pre-requisite courses, I had moved in with my mom and stepfather and I knew I would soon need to re-apply to the nursing program because again, I knew that was my calling. I re-applied and in a short time I found out I was accepted. I was over the moon happy and excited but scared at the same time. Shortly after that, my divorce was final. I then had six months before the semester would start. In a couple of months, I moved out of my mother and stepfathers' home and moved the girls and me into our apartment. Time went on and it was time to go to orientation for the nursing program. During orientation, one of the first things that were said was, "if you are working a full-time job, you are less likely to make it in this program." I immediately felt a pit in the bottom of my stomach. I am a single mother at that point with twin girls that are three years old and I had to work full time to provide for my family. I went home that night and I prayed, and I just asked God to guide me and order my steps. I knew that God would be with me every step of the way, and even though I was scared, anxious, and worried, I knew that regardless of the outcome this was my calling, and I would do everything in my power to succeed. I knew that quitting my job was not an option. Soon after, the semester started. I worked 8 am-5 pm Monday through Friday. I went to class Monday, Tuesday, Wednesday 5:30-9 pm and on Thursdays 5:30-9 pm for half of each semester, then I had clinical at the hospital every Saturday and Sunday from 6:30 am-5:30 pm. I am proud to say that I passed each semester. There was never a semester that I was in jeopardy of failing. If it wasn't for the support of my mom, stepfather, my ex-mother-in-law, and of course the Lord himself I don't know that I would have made it. During my last semester of nursing school, I met the man that would later become my second husband. In two years, I graduated with my associate degree in nursing. Not only did I graduate, but I also passed the state board exam on the first try. I was so amazed at all I had accomplished with all the obstacles thrown my way. Regardless, I was not going to let anything stop me from fulfilling my destiny.

The year I graduated nursing school; the economy had taken a huge hit. I could not find a job. Of course, my whole reason for going to nursing school was to become a neonatal nurse. Well, I tried, and I tried and could not get hired. In the back of my mind, I was thinking I am a single parent and I need to use my nursing degree to increase my income. I then started to apply for everything open. After a year, I landed my first job at an area hospital working on a cardiac unit. The only thing available was the night shift. My mother and stepfather once again stepped in to help me on the nights I went to work. Anybody that knows me, knows that I am not a night owl. I love my sleep. This was a huge shift for me. It was not going well. I was very emotional, I could not train my body to eat at night while I was working, I would fall asleep at the red light going home in the mornings as well. There was one day I would never forget. I would work, go home and sleep, and then wake up in time to get the girls off the school bus. They were in kindergarten. One day I picked them up, came home, and fixed them a snack. This was after working three nights in a row. I sat on the couch while they ate their snack. Well, unbeknownst to me, I fell to sleep. I slept for close to two hours when I jumped up and immediately started calling the twins names. I ran throughout the house and finally found them in a bathtub full of water play. Now that could have had a different outcome. They could have drowned, they could have left the house, they could have burned the apartment down, the list goes on of all the possibilities. I was so relieved that they were safe, however, I knew something needed to change. I could not continue to go on like this. Another issue being a brand-new nurse on this cardiac unit was that fear crept up inside of me again. Cardiac patients can be tough, and I was providing care for patients that had open heart surgery just a few days ago. Some of the patients would do well post-surgery, but then you had ones that had complications. That started to wear on me emotionally. I became afraid of death again. The thought of someone dying on my watch made me sick to my stomach. I loved what I was doing, but then there was that fear of death again creeping up inside of me. The very fear that I let talk me out of becoming a physician. I remember every shift repeating to myself the scripture II Timothy 1:7 For God hath not given us the spirit of fear, but of power, and love, and a sound mind. That did bring a calming presence over me when I said that scripture to myself. However, I began to become very anxious every time I was scheduled to work. I knew that with all of this going on, I needed to talk to someone. First, I went to a counselor regarding my fear of death. I did two sessions, but it was not working fast enough. I then asked to meet with my manager and my clinical educator. They were both amazing. They both listened to my concerns and both understood. At first, I thought, maybe if I switch to the day shift the normal hours will help with the anxiety. After speaking with my manager, that was not an option. As mentioned, the economy was not in a good place and there was a waiting list of people that wanted day shift. My manager set up a meeting with the director of cardiac services to see if there was another area in cardiac services that I may be able to transition to that would be less critical with a lesser chance of death. My manager told me she would hate to lose me because I was a very good nurse, but she understood what I was going through, and she felt I could be an asset to another area under cardiac services. We met with the director, and I was told there was nowhere else that I could work that I would not run into the same issues. The director felt I should stay put and work through it. I was crushed because for a split second, I had hope for a positive change. I continued to work nights on the same unit and tried to work through my issues. One day on my day off, I received a phone call from an area cardiology outpatient clinic. The office manager called stating she found my resume on monster jobs. One of the physicians needed a nurse because the previous nurse was moving away. I was asked if I could come in that day to interview. Of course, I went in to interview. I was told that the physician that needed a nurse was out of town for a week and they could not decide until the physician was back. I left there very optimistic and hopeful. I knew that could be an opportunity to turn my life around and get back to some normalcy. The night shift was becoming to wear on me worse and worse with my emotions. That very evening, I received a call back from the office manager stating she had spoken to the physician on the phone about me because she liked me so much and felt that I was a good fit for the position. The physician told her to go ahead and hire me. They wanted me to start right away. The same day I emailed my manager and asked to speak with her. I informed her that I was turning in my notice. She was very receptive and was happy for me that I had found something. I still speak with that manager to this day and she has been a great mentor to me over the years. I started my new job that very week and worked out my notice at that hospital for four weeks. I was exhausted; however, it was worth it to be able to make that change. I loved my new job. I learned a lot as a nurse. I felt guilty for not staying at the hospital and getting lots of medical-surgical experience, however it was a great change for my life as a person and as a mother. It was not what I initially went to nursing school for, however it worked for my life and I would not change anything about it. I felt very lucky to get that experience.

A little over a year later after starting my new, wonderful job, I married my second husband. Soon after I gave birth to my third child a baby girl. I initially went back to work after giving birth to her, but after about three months we decided I would stay home with her. I enjoyed being a stay-at-home mom, but I missed my patients and my career. I decided to enroll in an RN-BSN program while I was staying home with my kids. In December 2014, I graduated with a Bachelor of Science in Nursing. In 2015 I went back to work

PRN at the Cardiology practice I was working at before becoming a stay-at-home mom. Soon after, my marriage became rocky due to circumstances I will not discuss here. I was only working about 16 hours a week and I did not have my health insurance. There were no full-time jobs there. I then applied at the same area hospital I worked at as a new graduate in the float pool which was another PRN position. I was then working two PRN jobs. I needed full-time with benefits, but I could not find a job. Two months later, my husband and I separated. I applied for many full-time jobs and nothing was happening. No interviews, no calls, nothing. Finally, two months later, I had an interview at the hospital in the case management department. A week later I was offered the position. I was both excited and scared because honestly, I did not know what case managers do, but I felt comfortable because it was on the cardiac unit. I had to resign from both PRN positions. The cardiology practice was happy for me. I hated to leave that job because I loved everyone I worked with and loved my job; I just needed a full-time job. When I met with the manager of the float pool, she said that because I had not been in the position a full year I could not resign. There was no way I could work full-time Monday through Friday in the case management department and work two weekends a month in the float pool. I had to go to the human resources business partner to beg them to let me resign because I could not do all of that as a single parent of three kids. After about a week of meetings and negotiations, I could resign from the PRN float pool position. Finally, I could breathe a sigh of relief because in three weeks I would be starting a new full-time job with benefits and a pay increase so that I could provide for my girls. A year later, my second husband and I divorced. So here I am Bachelor of Science in Nursing, and a single parent of three girls working full-time as a Nurse Case Manager. Two years later, I became certified in case management.

Three years into being a nurse case manager, I love my job and what I am doing, however, it was not my calling. I aspired to be a family nurse practitioner. I investigated the nurse practitioner program at the school I went to for my bachelor's degree. I met with my manager about going to school. It would require me after the first year to have two weekdays off to do clinical for the program. My manager gave me her blessing and said that soon there will be a case management position starting in the Emergency Department which would be part-time and fewer hours so it would work out if I agreed to move to the Emergency Department. So, I agreed to move, and I started the family nurse practitioner program. A few months later it was time to make the transition to move to the Emergency Department. Unbeknownst to me, the part-time case management position in the Emergency Department was ten-hour rotating shifts from 6 am-4:30 pm one day and 2 pm-12:30 am one night a week. There was no way I could do that as a single parent neither time worked for me. I could not get the kids to school with the first shift and could not pick them up from school the second shift. Once again, my dreams were crushed. The only position I could take in the Emergency Department was one day off every other week 8 am-4:30 pm Monday through Friday. I then had to call my academic advisor because there was no way I could do the nurse practitioner program. Luckily the Master's in Nurse Education degree were the same classes I had already taken and it was clinical one day a week, so I changed my major. I spoke with my manager and she agreed to allow me to work 9 hours four days a week so that I could have one day off a week to complete clinical for the nurse education degree. In February 2019, I graduated with a Master's in Nurse Education. While it was not what I wanted, I was happy with the accomplishment. Soon after I started applying for master's level nursing jobs. I applied for ten jobs went on six interviews and was turned down for them all. I grew very tired and frustrated. I believe that was God's way of telling me that was not meant for me and to continue pursuing my purpose. I stopped applying for jobs and began to just pray and wait for the right opportunity to pursue my goal. A year later, COVID-19 hit my area and things began to shut down including schools. Many were forced to home-school their kids. Luckily, the twins were old enough to stay home with my little girl. I would work all day then come home to do schoolwork with the baby girl. I was exhausted. I knew that when it was time for the next school year to start if it was at home again, I had to make a change. When it came time for the next school year, it was home-school three times a week. Luckily there was a need for another case manager that worked weekends. I met with my manager and coordinator and they agreed that I could transition to Friday-Sunday twelve-hour shifts. With that transition, it allowed me to enroll in school again for the Family Nurse Practitioner Certificate program since I already have a master's degree. So that brings me where I am now. I have been homeschooling my baby girl, doing classes myself for the nurse practitioner program, and working every Friday-Sunday twelve-hour shifts. I am finally fulfilling my goal to be a nurse practitioner. While the road was not easy with lots of ups and downs, I am happy and thankful to soon live out my dream of being a nurse practitioner. Am I tired? Of course, I am. Is it stressful? Of course, it is. However, in the end, it will all be worth it. It took me so long to get here. With my support system and God, I have made it this far and I will not stop until I get to where I am supposed to be. Never give up on your calling, your dreams, and your aspirations. Keep pressing forward. It may be a long road, but at least you got to the finish line. It was not easy for me; however, I was not going to let anything be a crutch or stop me from getting to my purpose and my calling.

Racism

Racism is prejudice, discrimination, or antagonism against a person or people based on their membership in a particular racial or ethnic group, typically one that is a minority or marginalized. During my nursing career, living in the south, I have encountered racism. I have not and will not let that hinder my career. I treat everyone the same when I am caring for my patients regardless of their skin color, religious preference, or culture. However, I cannot say that I am always treated fairly because of the color of my skin. It breaks my heart that some people cannot look past my skin color and look at me as a person, a human being and treat me with respect and dignity.

The first encounter was when I was still working at a doctor's office when I first finished nursing school waiting to find a job at the hospital when the economy was down. One of my co-workers was busy with another patient so I decided to help her out and check in one of her patients for her provider. I checked in a middle-aged Caucasian man. I had never met this man before. I noticed that he was not very talkative and seemed very angry. His blood pressure was extremely high. So, I asked if he had taken his blood pressure medicine that day. He responded and said, "Yes I took my medicine my blood pressure is high because of you." I said, "excuse me?" He said, "black people make me angry, and because you touched me and took my blood pressure it caused my blood pressure to be high." I could not believe what had just happened. I did not know what to say to that. I took a couple of seconds to get my thoughts together then I said, "I am sorry you feel that way, but if you would like I can get someone else to come in and re-check your blood pressure." He then said, "I just want you to get out." I then left the room. With tears in my eyes, I told my co-worker what had transpired. She could not believe it. She said she would have never thought that patient would have acted that way. She went in to re-check his blood pressure and needless to say it was still elevated. He told her he did not want me to check him in anymore or come anywhere near him. That hurt my feelings. I could not believe that simply the color of my skin made him that angry. Not because I was rude or mean to him, but just the color of my skin. How can someone have so much hate in their heart due to skin color? We are all humans. We are all children of God. I am hated just because of my skin color. That was so upsetting. I looked for his name every day since then to be sure I did not have any other encounters with him.

The next encounter I had was when I was a new graduate at an area hospital. I walked into the room of a middle-aged Caucasian woman to introduce myself as her nurse for the night. As soon as I walked into the room, I introduced myself as her nurse for the night. She looked up at me and stated, "you are not my nurse tonight, but you can take my trash and clean up this nasty dirty room." I stated, "Ma'am, I am your nurse for tonight, but I will be glad to get environmental services to come in and empty your trash and tidy up your room." She then asked to speak to the person in charge. I grabbed the charge nurse, and she went to speak with the patient. The patient told the charge nurse she did not want me as her nurse and that she needed to be assigned to someone else. The charge nurse then switched with me and gave me one of her patients instead. I felt so humiliated. This lady did not even give me a chance. All because of the color of my skin. Even though she humiliated me, I remained calm and still treated her with respect. I did not let that get me down or make me act out of character.

It is so hard to believe that after all these years minorities are still dealing with racism. Regardless of how I have been treated, I will never let it change me as a person. I will still treat everyone regardless of their skin color or religious preference or cultural background with respect and dignity even if I do not get the same in return.

The Nursing Profession

In my opinion, the nursing profession is a very exciting and rewarding career. It is forever changing, and there will always be a need for it. There are so many different areas of nursing so one would never get bored. Whether you work at a doctor's office, nursing home, hospital, a research firm, and so forth, it will always be a rewarding career. I would like to see some changes made for the better for the nursing field. New nurses need mentors and lots of support. I feel that my new graduate experience would have been different if I had that mentor or person to help me fight through my issues. I would also like to see the nurse-to-patient ratios changed. I feel that patients could get better care and employers could retain more nurses if they changed the ratios. The current ratio in my area is 6:1 and sometimes more depending on staffing needs. This causes burnout and compassion fatigue in nurses. Nurses are stretched thin and find it hard to give excellent care and attention to all their patients when they have six patients. Hopefully in the future nurses can come together to fight for this change. During my Master's in Nurse Education degree, I did my project on PTSD in critical nurses. There are a lot of nurses that go through post-traumatic stress whether they are in critical care or on a medical-surgical unit. Managers need to recognize this and help get these nurses' help when they experience this.

My Passion

In January of 2022, I will be graduating from the nurse practitioner certificate program. Even though my reason for going into nursing was premature babies, at this time my passion and my goal is to see the health of my community changed for the better. I grew up in Wilmington, North Carolina. I have lived here all my life. I am passionate about my community and the place I have always called home. I know that some minorities do not have access to health care. I want to provide health care to those that have lost trust in the medical society, or who just do not have access to care whether it is due to finances or lack of health insurance. I know this will not happen quickly, but I will get there one day. I care about the health of my community and I want us to be healthy and live long lives.

I wrote this to share my story of resiliency. My advice to anyone reading this is to keep pressing forward. Regardless of what you may go through or what may happen don't let it be a crutch. Keep going. Get to the finish line. Obstacles will happen, but don't let them deter you. Don't let anything stop you from fulfilling your goals, dreams, purpose, or aspiration. In the bible Proverbs, 3:5-6 says, "Trust in the Lord with all your heart and lean not on your own understanding; in all your ways submit to him, and he will make your paths straight." I thank everyone that I have encountered in my life. You are all a part of my story in some way, and I could not have done any of this without you. Good or bad. I would not change anything about my life story because it all has made me who I am today. I would like to dedicate this to my strong mother that taught me to persevere, my stepdad that taught me to never give up, and my three beautiful girls. I love you.

Larnette Moore

Larnette Moore

BSN, RN

L arnette Larnette Moore is a registered nurse in N.C. She graduated with a Bachelor of Science Degree in Nursing from University of NC-Wilmington and will be completing her Master of Science Degree in Nursing Education, Summer, 2021 from Chamberlain University. She is a member of the North Carolina Nurses Association and American Nurses Association.

Larnette is celebrating 13 years in progressive care/ICU step-down, travel nursing, and cardiac surgical nursing. Larnette is a February 2020 Daisy Award winner for compassionate and extraordinary nursing in her current role as nurse case manager. Larnette will soon begin a new journey in her career as a clinical nurse educator.

Larnette is passionate about expanding diversity in nursing. Larnette chose to pursue a graduate degree in nursing education to influence and encourage persons of color to join, grow, succeed, and stay in the profession of nursing. Larnette plans to take her passion further by creating a mentoring program. Larnette hopes to inspire and mentor the next generation of young minority nurses into exceptional nurses. Larnette has been blessed throughout her career, with amazing influences from seasoned nurse veterans. Larnette has taken the wisdom imparted to her, education, and experience to ready herself for a seat at the leadership table. In doing so, she hopes to bring diversity to the highest levels of the nursing professions decision making ladder. In her free time, Larnette spends time at the beach to relax, reflect, and release.

From Anger to Acceptance

Anger

"Calm down why are you so angry?" Those were the words spoken to me by a white male coworker. For months I experienced listening to a white female coworker openly express her thoughts about a variety of topics that were offensive and inappropriate to be discussing in the workplace. I never confronted her. I sat at my desk and did my work. The white male coworker sat in the next cubicle over from me. He approached me at the copier and commented that he was "sick and tired of hearing her yapping." I agreed with him and walked back to my desk. I continued to endure the agony of listening to her speak so openly and freely about anything and everything.

One day, shortly after Trump won the Republican nomination for president of the United States, the white female coworker was sharing how she had talked to her son about "being white in America". She shared that "there is no excuse to be a white man in American and not be successful. If you are a white man in America and you are poor, it is because you are lazy." Later in her speech she stated "The one that has it the worst is a black woman. You could not pay me to be a black woman in America. This country doesn't give a s**t about black women." She mentioned that this country was not ready for a female president and that is why "Obama got into the white house." She went on to say, "the white man is the top dog, and the black woman is the underdog." I wish I could say I was surprised by the words that I was hearing, but I was not. What surprised me was how quiet the room got. It was as if everyone knew she had crossed the line, but no one had the guts to say it.

I heard enough, and I was over it. I decided rather than confront her and risk getting myself in trouble, if the situation escalated, I chose to send an email to the manager and practice administrator. I shared exactly what was said and how I felt about it. I also named everyone present during the time the inappropriate things were being said. I did not receive any response from either person. Each day I continued to work in an environment that was extremely uncomfortable.

I was returning from break walking towards my desk, and the white male coworker walked up to me. He let me know he had spoken with our manager. He informed me the manager asked him about the incident from my email. I was happy to hear that the manager had asked this person. I was certain this person would speak up for me. I was certain he would tell the truth and detail everything he had heard. Boy, was I a fool? I asked him "Okay so what did you say?" He looked at me with this look as if he did not want to speak. I had a puzzled look on my face. I asked him again "Did you tell what you heard? Did you tell all the mess she says? He answered me and said "I don't want to get involved. I don't really think she means any harm. I said I didn't think she was being malicious." I could not believe what I was hearing. I said "Are you serious? You have got to be kidding me? What do you mean, 'you don't want to get involved,' YOU ARE INVOLVED!" I began to raise my voice at him. This was not the time to be silent. I thought he was an ally. I was extremely let down and disappointed.

It was that moment he responded, "calm down, why are you so angry?" Those words played repeatedly in my head. I looked him in the face and told him "don't you dare call me angry! You have no right to make me out to be the angry black woman. I have every right to be angry." I walked away and went to my desk. I could not focus on my work. I was visibly upset to the point, another coworker asked if I were, okay? I asked if she would cover me for the remainder of the day and I went home.

Before this incident occurring, there had been another incident that occurred in the office- which was also extremely inappropriate. During a morning team huddle, the staff noticed a homophobic slur had been written on the communication board. It was immediately erased, but everyone was shocked to see it written. Later that same day, the practice administrator called a staff meeting. Noticeably upset before the meeting started. The administrator let everyone know that what had occurred would not be tolerated in that work environment. The administrator let everyone know due diligence would be done to find out who committed the act and there would be consequences. The administrator expressed that everyone was to feel safe and included in the work environment and that there was zero tolerance for discrimination or inequality in our work environment. Hearing all of this said gave me the confidence to send the email to the manager and administrator about what was going on in my work area.

I was confused and disappointed when I did not experience the same passionate response to my situation as I witnessed was carried out when the homophobic slur incident occurred. Why is it so that, someone writes an inappropriate word about gay people and there is an immediate response, but I am a black woman, the only full-time black nurse in my work area reporting that I am being offended almost daily by comments being made by a white coworker, and nothing! Absolutely nothing was said in response to my email from the administrator to me. I eventually heard back from the manager. The manager shared that the incident had been investigated but there was not enough feedback from the staff that substantiated my claims. The manager shared that a conversation had been had with the white female coworker. She was instructed to "talk less and work more." I knew things would not change. I felt discouraged, defeated, and voiceless. I wondered if the intent was to break my spirit and drive me out. In a way, they won, because that is exactly what I did. I decided it was time to find a new place of employment. It was more important for me to protect my peace. The stress was beginning to take a toll on my health. I felt my disdain for my job was affecting my attitude and job performance. I hated going to work. I eventually transferred to another location in the organization.

Those words he used triggered me. By the time this incident had occurred, I had been a nurse for seven years. I had experienced many instances of workplace microaggressions throughout those seven years. In many instances, they were so thinly veiled, that I questioned myself. I wondered was I being overly sensitive? Why wasn't any of my black coworkers saying anything? Was I the only one noticing what was going on?

Early in my nursing career, I had a heated exchange with a white nurse. She asked me to watch her patients while she took a break. She left the unit and did not return for over an hour. I had a heavy assignment. I had sick patients and did not have time to manage her patients and mine for such a long length of time. Typically, when you take a break, you make sure all your patients have been checked on, everyone's needs are met, and everyone should be fine until you return. She did not do that. While I am caring for my patients, I keep being called for things her patients needed. She returned to the unit and did not immediately let me know she was back. She stood at the nurse's station talking while I was running around trying to manage patient care on both our patients. I walked past the nurses 'station and heard her laughing. I called her name and immediately walked to her and passed her work phone to her. I told her "in the future do your work before you go off the floor. You left a mess for me to clean up." She responded back to me and the two of us started having an exchange.

The exchange escalated and ended when she made a threat. The charge nurse intervened at that moment and told both of us that was enough. The charge nurse reported both of us to the nurse manager, however before I was called to the manager's office the white nurse had already gone and told her side of the story. I reported to the manager's office to discuss what happened. The white nurse reported I yelled at her and threatened her. I admitted I was upset because of the way she left her patients and returned over an hour later. I told her "I did not get loud until she started getting loud with me." I said "I did not, however, threaten her. In fact, it was the other way around." The manager informed me she believed me, and she was not happy that we behaved the way we did out in the open at the nurse's station. The white nurse attempted to report me to human resources stating she felt unsafe working with me. She was the one that escalated the situation instead of taking responsibility for her actions she chose to play the victim. Had I done what she had done, I would have been written up or worse. As a black nurse, I always feel I must work twice as hard as my white counterparts, yet I still do not receive the same recognition or credit for what I do. I always feel like I must prove myself worthy. Meanwhile, the white nurses can be lazy and have a poor work ethic and be promoted to leadership positions.

A few years later I had another incident with a white charge nurse. I would continuously be given heavier assignments than some of my white counterparts. If we were short-staffed and had to take an extra patient, I was sure to be one of the nurses that would have to pick up an extra patient. I noticed this charge nurse was being unfair in the way she made the nurse assignments. One day I volunteered to help and picked up an extra shift. I had worked my four shifts, and this was my fifth day in a row. I requested the day before to have the same patients because I had been with those patients for the last four days. When I came in the next day, my assignment was changed. When I questioned why my assignment was changed, I was told another nurse (white nurse) assignment was too heavy and it needed to be broken up. I said, "okay well I am sorry for that nurse, however, this is an extra shift, I have worked the last four days with these patients, I know them, and I requested to have my same patients back." The charge nurse told me "oh well, we do not always get what we want." I was so upset I could not speak. I walked away.

Later that day, the charge nurse called me to the desk to give me medication for a patient. I walked up to her took the medication and walked away. She reported me to the manager and said I was "rude and being disrespectful." Once again, I had to go see the manager. This was a different manager from the previous one. This white manager did not give me the benefit of the doubt. She started by saying she "would not tolerate disrespectful behavior from staff", and she informed me of what she expected of the staff. I denied what I was being accused of. She told me she was "having a hard time believing me because of my body language." She then went on to say, that to keep me out of trouble in my career, I would need to learn to be "less aggressive and gentler." She advised that a smile would carry me a long way and to be more aware of my tone and body language. She told me she knew I was a "sweetheart" but without getting to know me, "because of my stature, I could be a bit intimidating from my appearance." As a black woman and a black nurse, I police my tongue, modulate my voice, choose my words carefully, meanwhile my white counterparts are not doing the same. They say whatever they choose to say without fear of consequence. How do you respond to that?

Although I had been a nurse a few years at that point, I still did not have the confidence in myself that I should have had. I did not stand up for myself the way I should have. All I wanted was to be successful in my role as a nurse, many of the other black nurses, seem to not want to make themselves a target. Many of them seem to want to blend in so they chose to grin and bear. If I wanted to have success and longevity in this profession, I had a choice, I could learn to play the grin and bear game, I could become one of those "token black folk" that knows how to make the white people feel comfortable around them, or I could be true to myself. I chose the latter. But who was I? What exactly was being true to myself mean? I felt like Oprah Winfrey in The Color Purple, "All my life I had to fight." True to myself for me, means owning everything about myself that makes me the dope, black queen that I am.

Acceptance

One of my favorite scenes in the movie The Color Purple is when Celie, the character played by Whoopi Goldberg leaves Mister, a character played by Danny Glover. In the scene, she comes to self-acceptance. Overcoming all the adversity, prejudices, and hardships she has endured over her life, Celie tells him, "I'm poor, black; I may even be ugly. But dear God! I'm here! I'm here!" This was a pivotal moment in her life. She gained her voice and took her power back from him. I relate to that scene in my career and as a black woman.

Throughout my career, I desired to have someone take me under their wings and mentor me to guide me. I sought out those with the wisdom and experience for advice and guidance. Developing a strong network of black women to surround me. Women that are trustworthy and honest can provide me with feedback to help navigate me. Unfortunately, I was unsuccessful in my quest to find a said network of peers. I found myself becoming resentful and depressed. I was resentful every day that I faced another long day of working in a position that I felt I was greater than.

I appreciate every nursing position I have had. Each role taught me something and helped me to grow. However, I reached a point where I knew I needed and wanted more complex responsibility, more autonomy, a greater role. I pursued opportunities for promotion and/or leadership where I could have influence or authority to make meaningful changes, but instead, I became a threat to the status quo in the workplace. I started questioning my abilities, although I knew that racial bias was likely the reason I was being held back. Despite being labeled "An angry black woman" and facing many challenges because of microaggression in my career, I refuse to give up. I have been underutilized, overlooked, ignored, lied to, lied on, rejected, and yet every day, I continue to show up and excel with passion and a commitment to my profession. I know who I am, I know whose I am, and I know what I am not. I am black, educated, and I am here. Shirley Chisholm (1968), said: "If they don't give you a seat at the table, bring a folding chair."

As I continue to demonstrate high levels of confidence and performance in my nursing roles, I am challenged with barriers to career advancement. I am committed to professional development I am a natural-born leader. My presence commands attention, I will not apologize for that. I will continue to be assertive and demand the respect I give to others. I will not allow the opinions and insecurities of others to diminish my achievements, my hard work, my education, my experience, my voice, my creativity, and my influence. I will not diminish who I am so that others will feel comfortable in my presence.

God created us all for a purpose. We must seek to discover our purpose. I have a responsibility to my community. I am passionate about professional growth. Education is something that cannot be taken from me. I believe professional advancement is critical. My community needs more nurses that look like me in leadership positions, in academia, boardrooms, and legislature. Black nurses are essential to providing the Black community with better health care. Nurses like me can provide opportunities for the black community to receive quality care from people who look like and can relate to them. The future of nursing needs more black nurse educators in the classrooms, that is why I am pursuing my master's degree in nursing education. I will continue to seek out and develop strong relationships with other resilient black nurses.

Creating a strong network of peers who understand the struggles we as black nurses face in our profession, so we may rally around one another to uplift, support, inspire, each other. Preparing for the road ahead, my future looks promising. I know that there will always be challenges that I must face in my profession as a black woman. I will face those challenges head-on because that is where growth and strength will form. My advice to all my black queens is to leave the room better than you found it.

Cecilia Lacy

Cecilia Lacy

RN

Cecilia Lacy Cecilia McIlwain is a Registered Travel Nurse who is currently based in Concord, North Carolina. She is the daughter of Bishop Michael C. McIlwain and Reverend Dr. Teresa McIlwain of Charlotte, North Carolina. Cecilia graduated from Northwest School of the Arts in Charlotte North Carolina where she studied music and dance. After attending UNC-Charlotte for her pre nursing studies, she received her Diploma in Nursing from Mercy School of Nursing in 2006 and is presently an active and proud nurse member of the National Black Nurses Association, North Carolina Nurses Association and American Nurses Association.

Cecilia is celebrating fourteen years in medical surgical nursing and has enjoyed working in acute care and the outpatient settings. Nursing is a passion for her because she enjoys teaching patients and their families, loves to travel, and is always excited and eager to learn more and meet new people. Cecilia is so proud to be the mother of two daughters, Seanna Lacy (10), and Shanelle Lacy (9).

Journey to Divine Destiny

I am a proud, educated, black, resilient nurse and I own and appreciate my journey. It has not been easy, but it has taught me so much and has been worth every lesson and gift that it has given me. One encounter with a nurse, as a child, changed my life forever. It jump-started my desire to become a nurse and would be the catalyst to start me on my journey to my divine destiny. I grew from a young child dreaming to a teen on the path to nursing, to a nursing student, and ultimately would become the nurse I always dreamed and desired that I could be. I had challenges along the journey, and I have walked through tough situations, but they taught me how to be resilient and gave me a burning passion for the art of nursing and the desire to teach and encourage other young men and women to reach for the stars and be a powerful and brilliant nurse one day.

As a child, my dream was to grow up and become a nurse one day. It all started with a visit to a local hospital as a child of about eight years old. A nurse greatly inspired me. My father was the pastor of a church in Indianapolis, Indiana and our family would often go to the hospital after church and visit members there. I remember a particular time when we visited an older woman from the church. As we entered the room, she was lying in bed resting. My father walked to her bedside to talk and pray with her. As they were conversing, a young woman walked into the room and stood by her beside patiently. She wore a soft smile and a crisp white top and pants, and white shoes. I remember all the white stood out in such a way that I thought she reminded me of an angel. She spoke to the lady in bed in a calm soft voice, gently tucked her in, and made her comfortable. I could not stop watching her. I heard the sincerity in her voice, saw the compassion in her eyes, and witnessed the gentle touch she had, and it drew me in. I knew during that encounter that this was what I wanted to do when I grew up. I had a desire to meet new people, discover their stories, and touch them in a caring way that would help heal their hearts and hurts. This is when I began to dream.

My nursing journey started twenty-four years ago when I was a curious thirteen-year-old seventh-grader, looking to learn more about nurses and what nursing was all about. My mother was a chaplain for a hospital in Charlotte, North Carolina where we lived. She heard about their candy striper volunteer program for teens, and I signed up. I was extremely excited for the opportunity to take a peek into the world of medicine and nursing and see what they did, how they interacted with patients, and how nurses and doctors worked together. I was so eager to learn how the healing process happens. I had the best years working as a candy striper at the hospital. We were able to deliver flowers to sick patients and brand-new mothers. I will never forget the smell of fresh flowers in the flower room that was waiting to be delivered to patients. We were also allowed to pass ice, drinks, snacks, newspapers, cards, and help the nurses and unit clerks with making paper packets for the patient charts. These were what some would call small tasks, but it all meant the world to me just to be there. I loved the way the patients would smile when they saw me, a young, brown-skinned girl walk in their rooms with the signature candy cane-colored dress and a big smile, with flowers, gifts, or snacks for them. They were so pleasant and always grateful for a visit. I felt I knew I was supposed to be there. It felt so right. I was a candy striper until my eleventh-grade year and then decided I was interested in shadowing with nurses on the units at the hospital. I decided to join the Nursing Explorers program through my school. Explorers were high school teens who wanted to shadow and learn more about professionals in a variety of career programs. The Nursing Explorers shadowed nurses on the units, wrote reports, sat in sessions with nurses where we could ask questions about the profession, and worked on projects to help us learn more about all nursing had to offer. This was an incredible program, and I will always be grateful for the opportunity to connect with and learn from some amazing nurses.

After graduating high school, I enrolled in the pre-nursing program at UNC-Charlotte. I had two great years completing all of my prerequisites. The closer I got to apply for the nursing school, the more excited and energized I became. It was all starting to come together, and I was closer to my dream. The first semester I have the opportunity to apply for the nursing program, I was advised there were around 300 candidates, and I was placed on the waiting list. Instead of having to possibly wait another semester to enter the program, I decided to apply for the Mercy School of Nursing Program and start in their summer session. I was blessed to get accepted and officially transferred to Mercy School of Nursing, one of the first schools to open in the state of North Carolina. I was so excited to be one step closer. It was a major accomplishment.

Although the journey through nursing school was a challenge, I am so very grateful for the opportunity to have attended and graduated from a very historic nursing school program that had been open since 1906. I graduated in 2006, on the one-hundredth anniversary of the school. It was an amazing milestone. Walking the path through this program gave me the preparation, confidence, tools, and support that I needed to be a successful nursing student and nurse. It was an incredible foundation for my now fourteen-year nursing journey. One thing I particularly enjoyed and was motivated by while I was in school was the diversity of the staff. We had male, female, black, white, and Hispanic nursing instructors. This was very new to me and I loved it. Until that time, I had only met a few black nurses. To see them excited, empowered, encouraging, and excited about nursing, and willing to guide us to a path of success was exactly what I needed. They uplifted us and each other and it showed me that I was right where I needed to be and that I did belong. I graduated in December 2006 and passed my boards and became an official registered nurse in 2007. It was a dream fulfilled and I had finally walked the journey and made it to my place of divine destiny. I was on top of the world and so excited about all of the possibilities that were ahead of me in nursing. I knew my opportunities were endless and I could continue to dream. Nursing has so much to offer.

As I reflect on all of the amazing opportunities and joyful moments along my journey, I am also reminded of the challenges I had to overcome along the way. As I look back, I see how they helped me grow, stretch, learn, and become the person that I am today. As a young teen candy striper, I recall being one of the only black young ladies in my program at the time. I never knew or understood why that was, but I was proud to be there. As I look back, I believe it was because young black students had limited interest and exposure to programs like that, for various reasons. I was excited to share with my friends that I was a candy striper at the hospital because I aspired to be a nurse one day. The common response was usually the question "why?", because I had to give up one or two evenings a week to go volunteer. I saw it as a privilege to be there, but I felt pressure at the same time. I felt as though I was often being watched because I was different. I felt like I stood out in the crowd because I was a young black female. I felt the pressure present myself without flaw because I didn't want to make "us" (black people) look bad. I felt I could be myself most times, but sometimes, it felt as though it wasn't enough. When I started the Explorers program, I was paired with several very kind and lovely Caucasian nurses that I would shadow. They were great and I am so grateful for all they taught me. I did have a desire deep down to also rotate and shadow with a black nurse as well. I never had that opportunity and felt I missed out on exposure to another window and view into what nursing would be like from their perspective.

As I look back on my college experience leading to nursing school, there is one particular event that could have changed my journey forever. I applied for the Nursing Program at UNC-Charlotte and went to speak to my counselor about the path to the program. She told me that there was a high volume of students applying to the nursing school that semester. I asked her if I was put on the waiting list, what would be the process to wait it out or apply for the next enrollment period. Without hesitation, she said " maybe nursing isn't for you", "maybe you can take an art class and get your GPA up and become a Biology major instead". I was so surprised and shocked. This was my guidance counselor, and she was counseling me away from my goal and dream. I wondered if she felt I was not good enough to be a registered nurse. I had this dream in my heart for many years, and it caught me off guard to hear those words. I was hurt. I recall gathering my composure and telling her " I am going to be a nurse because that's what I came here to do", " I will do whatever it takes". Her hurtful comments followed me through most challenges I had along my path to nursing. Those words would play over and over in my head when I didn't do well on an exam or when it was a challenge to grasp a particular topic in class in nursing. It even followed me into nursing. They would play in my head like a bad tape, if I had a rough shift or if I had a patient who was unkind to me. "Am I worthy?" and "Do I belong here?", planting seeds of doubt about my place in nursing. With the help of wonderful nurse mentors, family, and friends that supported me, I grew to a place where I realized it was only words and I could replace that negative tape in my head with positive and encouraging affirmations about myself because I knew who I was, and I knew who God created me to be. " I am skilled, I am blessed, I am favored, I am here because this is my gift, I will succeed". I changed my life.

As I started working full-time as a registered nurse (RN), I realized there would be more challenges along my journey that I had not encountered before. I found that some patients did not seem to be comfortable with the idea of having a black nurse, some staff were not very receptive to a black nurse in leadership, and it was initially difficult to make connections with other nurses on the units I worked. I have been asked many times in my career, "So you are my nurse?"," I thought you were my nurse aide" or " so you are really a registered nurse?". These comments were usually accompanied by puzzled facial expressions. This would even occur after I formally introduced myself to the patient or their family as their nurse. I received these comments from people of all backgrounds and races.

It puzzled me that these were such common phrases that I heard. I could not quite grasp why it was so difficult for people to see the possibility of me being very capable of being a nurse, especially upon first meeting me. Initially, it would bother me every time it happened, because I felt I had to once again justify and prove why I was good enough and capable of being their nurse and doing a great job at it. It took me back to the feelings I had as that candy striper striving to prove myself along the way. As I started to grow and mature as a nurse, I realized that I could change my feelings and attitude towards the responses and the people behind them. I was empowered to overcome the thoughts that I was not enough. I started to use those moments as an opportunity to teach and educate my patients and their families about why I loved being a nurse and a little bit about my history with the current department I worked in. I found that for the most part, my patients and their families were very receptive and even encouraging at times. They were open to sharing and would give feedback and even tell me about their family members who were nurses and how they admired their work in the medical field. It was a blessing to use something that could have been a roadblock, to being a stairstep to elevate how I thought of myself as a nurse. It definitely boosted my confidence.

I have worked as a nurse in many different settings such as acute care hospitals, nursing homes, and outpatient clinics. I found at times; it was a challenge for some staff to follow the leadership of a black nurse. I noticed as my counterparts gave instructions, delegated tasks, and took leadership roles in the department, they were received better than I was. Many times, I was one of a couple of back nurses on the unit. I started the unit-based council on the first unit I worked in as a nurse and was a member of the nurse congress, but it was extremely difficult to get my coworkers to attend meetings, review the agendas I created or even follow through with new policies I was responsible for teaching about and initiating on our unit. Those were difficult times for me because I put forth a lot of effort to be a good leader and I could never get feedback about why I was not being received as such. As a seasoned nurse, I have learned that it is my job to put forth the effort and be the best leader I can, engage with all staff, whether they receive me or not, be open-minded and aware that people have different perspectives, and let my work speak for me. This has been a success in many settings that I have worked in. I now feel appreciated. My coworkers respect my work and efforts, communication is open-ended, and as my co-workers have come to know me, they are pleasantly surprised that I may not be the person they initially anticipated I would be. I'm a passionate nurse on my journey.

I now appreciate the challenges along my journey, because I have learned from them and have been able to grow and overcome in many ways. They have taught me how to be resilient, strong, wise, and the best example that I can be to other young men and women that choose to walk this same journey to nursing. I am so very grateful for my nursing journey and every step along the way. Every step was a steppingstone to becoming someone greater and wiser in the field. I hope to be a light and an inspiration to those that question themselves and ask if they have what it takes to pursue the journey to lead them to their dreams. Not just nursing, but whatever they have a passion to do. I hope they can remember that little girl from my story, sitting in the hospital room, watching with wonder and dreaming of who she could be one day. I hope they remember the little girl who was inspired by the light and love that she saw in one person and saw how they could shine. We all have a destiny and a dream to chase. It's that thing that drives us to be the best we can be. Be encouraged to walk that journey to your divine destiny with God's grace, patience, pride, love for yourself, respect for others, kindness, gentleness, while remaining humble. Go and be great! Change the world, one step of your journey at a time.

Carolyn Burke Davis

Carolyn Burke Davis

LPN

Carolyn Carolyn Davis has over 40 years' experience in Healthcare. She received her BS degree in Biology and Health Education from UNC Fayetteville State University. She has worked numerous career paths in Nursing and Education.

She worked as a travel nurse in various specialties throughout the country and most recently in New York Metro during the beginning of the current pandemic. She has most recently completed assignments in North Carolina where she presently resides. She currently works as a Health Care Ambassador in the Raleigh-Durham area.

Her passion is educating people to make better decisions about their healthcare and quality of life. It would always anger her to hear a patient say, "whatever you say doc". Providers sometimes take advantage of this response leaving a patient with a less than desirable outcome. Just being informed is not good enough! As a care giver for her parents and others, she has found that asking questions and exploring options can produce significantly better outcomes. Unfortunately, everyone doesn't always get to make choices and you can't make good choices without knowledge.

As healthcare professionals, we have the responsibility of empowering our communities through education and health promotions. Advocating for better healthcare with our patients, our family and in our community starts with us, we have an integral role in eliminating racial health disparities. When she is not traveling, she enjoys growing succulents and spending time with family and all of her friends whom she has grown to love as family.

Ms. Davis will dedicate her story to her mother Lucille and her Aunt Ella Mae, who have both been examples of faith and love throughout her journey.

From Darkness to Light

Finding Light

My nursing career will always be with me even when I don't have to hit the time clock anymore. My career has been totally transformational. When I look back to where I was, with only a glimmer of hope, not knowing where I was going or what was before me, I am consumed with pride and amazement. There was always that glimmer of hope, that light that lets me know I'm on the right path.

Two of the most valuable things I have learned about my culture are one, survival will never be easy, and two, you got to keep rising until you see light. For me, that meant rising above disappointments, disrespect, racism, and injustice. For a societal change, it means speaking up, standing up, and being fearless about injustices that affect all ethnic groups. It's never been about one group; it's always been about all groups. As for me, throughout my career it's been about people, people of all races, creeds, and colors inflicting wounds of oppression and inequalities upon each other and the healthcare field is not exempt.

My training as a combat medic in the US Army strengthened me physically and mentally for all the various positions I've held throughout my career. I am proud and blessed to have served with such a diverse group. The experience of working beside people of different cultures and backgrounds has broadened my horizons, boosted my self-awareness, self-esteem and gave me the confidence I needed to seek new opportunities.

Pursue Light □

When I decided to move to New York I knew I needed to see myself as someone who stood out. I updated my resume often to fit the different job descriptions. Hopefully, they would get past the age discrimination and see what I had to offer. My age became more of a deterrent than the locs on my head.

Your life can be as good as your mindset. You do your best when you feel your best. Never allow someone else to decide your destiny, especially an establishment whose goals don't reflect your goals. You will be judged by your skin color or the Locs on your head, but don't let that deter you. Some of my best job offers happened while wearing my Locs. I had friends and family suggest wearing a wig or cutting my Locs off for an interview. A good interview comes with confidence, not deception. A good job experience comes with an employer that values you and your talent and one that is not blinded by the Locs on your head.

Your work experiences can be more valuable than the initials behind your name. Explore different opportunities, take risks if needed but remember it takes light to grow. My many experiences as a student, a nurse, and an educator have made me more aware of the importance of networking and resourcing collectively to bring about change. All people aren't bad and there are enough good people in the world to make a difference.

I attended a technical college for LPN school. My nursing class began with 26 students, at graduation, there were only 13 students. I saw others with great potential become crushed under the pressures of discrimination and unfair grading practices which ultimately led to expulsion. Every semester we wondered who's going next? It was very difficult for people of color to become a nurse on merit alone and getting into an RN program was very seldom discussed. I among other students of color were persuaded to enroll in the LPN program because some advisors thought we weren't RN material or that our failure on state boards would negatively impact the school rating. No matter how hard I studied or excelled in clinical performance, every semester I remained a C student.

At my pinning ceremony, the person that was awarded the highest score on the state board exams only scored 3 points higher than me, however, there was no honorary mention of second place. I had lost all trust in the system, wondering why I was the spared token, the only black to graduate out of my class. I wondered how I was a C student every semester, finally getting an A in clinicals the last semester and now the second-highest scorer on the state board.

After a year in my first nursing position, I tried to enroll in the RN program at the same school multiple times and was told I scored too low on the entry exam and they needed me to take a year of remedial classes. I was stunned with disbelief and determined not to allow this institution, which I had very little respect for, to determine my fate.

Friction causes light

Just because you see a light, that doesn't mean you know where you are going. Your response to your experiences counts 90% toward moving forward. My first nursing experience was on a pediatrics unit, which is my favorite specialty before critical care. That was the one place I got to feel the love. If only I could have taken all the children, I fell in love with at home! As long as children came in and got better, it was rewarding but watching an infant struggle for life and then die was very disheartening. It would just devour my energy for days!

My first job in critical care was rather traumatizing. I was young and inexperienced, living in Texas at the time. I was anxious to begin work and finally, after many applications, I got a call from the Catholic hospital. I went in for an interview and was offered a position in the neurosurgical ICU. I was shocked, there must be a mistake, this is not what I applied for, I have never worked in an intensive care unit before, and this was frightening. I asked to be considered for another position, the nun sternly rejected my request stating this was the only job that met my qualifications and proceeded with the job description and responsibilities. I can remember feeling scared, walking into that unit, the ventilators, the alarms, everyone around me speaking Latin or Spanish, but then thinking because of the religious affiliation, it can't be too bad. The unit consisted of 14 beds; I was one of two LVNs who would assist the sisters as needed. I only understood what they needed me to hear and that was very little. Most of the patients were on life support and all required total care. I was taught suctioning, catheterizations, and enteral feedings by very strict and high standards. I was racially profiled to do all the heavy lifting and cleaning. I needed to work, and I worked in fear of reprimand every day. I didn't choose this job; it had chosen me! I endured for three months and completed a two-week notice. If you don't learn from your mistakes you tend to keep making the same mistakes over and over.

I later moved to Atlanta and worked on a medical-surgical floor in a large teaching hospital. There were very little or no blacks in specialty units or leadership positions. People of color could only be found only in the darkest places in the establishment. Within those dark hallways, were some very hard-working nurses of many years with no hope of promotion or reassignment.

The work environment was oppressive, and the issues of the day were usually induced by a plantation mentality that consumed the organization from the floor up. Ridiculous work schedules, discriminating work assignments, dress code restrictions, and lack of support from management impacted the lives of workers and their families. I think back on all the missed opportunities for advancement, the missed family gatherings, birthdays, holidays, etc. that were stolen from me and my coworkers due to an unequal playground at the nurses' station.

There was always the few among us that would be sensitive to the obvious discrimination in assignments and work schedules. We would buddy up on difficult assignments or make adjustments on the "down-low". It's hard to believe, even now as I look back, we had some supervisors that did not want some of us to work together. If discovered, you would sometimes get floated to other areas or your schedules would be changed.

The majority of the nurses were consumed with unresolved work-related traumas. I can remember being pulled to work on another unit. The staff seemed very emotionally and physically strained due to the limited resources and the very difficult patient assignments. I listened compassionately to one despairing story after another as I struggled to do my best, helping others and completing my assignment. Nonetheless, it was reported to the supervisor that I wanted to sit around talking all night and the next time send them somebody that's used to working. I was rather shocked that a supervisor was saying these words. I was slow to respond, almost speechless when the supervisor shrugged off and said not to worry, she understands what happens down there you won't have to go down there again, and she will remember them the next time they ask for help. I found myself unable to grasp what happened and it bothered me. Had I spent an entire shift slaving and thinking I had made a difference? Had I lent my sympathetic ear to the enemy? What is this supervisor thinking?

I later spoke to one of the nurses I had worked with on that unit. She explained that management didn't care what happened down there, we just show up and do what we are going to do and go home, you came down there trying to do something different and people don't like that. I never thought that my nursing was different or that it would ever offend anyone. This wasn't only about the workers on that unit, it was also about the establishment, the workers seemed to be reacting to past experiences and feelings of hopelessness. Relentless oppression breeds discord between workers because they know leadership is not interested in their concerns. The staff was segregated, and the struggle is real.

Everything happens for a reason. Was I suffering from an illusion of the textbook version of Nursing 101? Am I being a little naive to think that all nurses are Florence Nightingale and all nursing departments function on the same principles? Nonetheless, it was at this point, very early in my career that I decided that I needed to be more serious about job decisions. Job decisions build resumes, and the content of resumes is used to judge one's worth or abilities. I also realized that I was naive about the profession, hospitals don't always take care of nurses and nurses don't always take care of nurses.

I did not want to get stuck in an oppressive situation that would change who I am or hinder my growth. Moving forward I would use more wisdom in accepting jobs, not taking whatever job is offered but will explore other possibilities and opportunities. We don't always know what we want but usually know where we are, so if you know where you are and you are not feeling inner peace, make that move! I became a fearless job seeker; I would shock myself at times. I applied for jobs, everyone else thought I wouldn't get. I never had a problem getting jobs, just finding one that would challenge me to the next level.

Growth comes with courage

Taking nurses out of caps and whites was almost as controversial as taking prayer and the pledge of allegiance out of schools. Some of the most skilled and dedicated nurses were judged by the stripes on their caps, the nursing school they attended, the color of their hair and skin. It was easy to see as you scrolled through different departments where the lines were drawn.

Even though caps and starched whites shouldn't define whether you are a good or bad nurse, they symbolized a system of values for nurses which includes dedication, honesty, wisdom, and faith. Seems like when caps went away so did the importance of displaying our value system. Many organizations required registered nurses to wear white uniforms but chose dull ugly colored uniforms for other staff. Some of us complained but as with everything else, not enough of us so our complaints went ignored by management. There are always the cowards who refuse to be a part of the process. Proclaiming "what difference does the color of the uniform make? My response is, if it doesn't make any difference why aren't we allowed to choose?

Everyone that has a soul responds to certain colors in certain ways. For me, the restricted colors symbolized racial bias and oppression and the constant reminder of who was in charge. All subtle acts of oppression need to be exposed and that exposure can also be subtle. Nurses eventually started a revolution for colored uniforms, everyone wearing their favorite colors and what matched their skin tones and hair color. They formed their sense of identity with matching shoes and accessories. This confirmed my belief about the colors.

I was fortunate to have spent most of my years in emergency medicine. I enjoyed working in scrubs because they were all the same color. We were all respected as a valued part of the team. Of course, that didn't change the color of my skin, but it was one step in the right direction. Now when I entered a room to perform a procedure or to start an IV, I wasn't mistaken as the housekeeper or assumed to be incompetent.

Faith and Determination

Critical care is challenging, and I loved it! It's like a race against time to produce some positive outcomes for some very sick people. When you are at the bedside of your patient with a doctor telling the family, we will see how it goes the next 24 hours and you are responsible for that patient the next 12 hours and the patient and family stares over at you, like can we trust her? Situations similar to this arise pretty often and my response is usually a reassuring nod. By now, others doubting me has become fuel for my soul.

No, I'm not a miracle worker but I believe in Grace, technology, and medicine. It takes attention to detail and teamwork to ensure a patient gets the best care possible. You have got to trust yourself and show confidence to gain trust from patients and co-workers. Yes, it's going to take a lot of work, which means volunteering to help others and bring open to learning new technology.

Working under pressure, that was every day, things could drastically change from one second to the next. I developed that "gut feeling " about most of my patients and I was usually right. The responsibility for hemodynamic monitoring and reporting to doctors promptly was very stressful and all doctors weren't so nice.

Some of the patients in my care were very difficult even though you tried your best to be supportive and reassuring, Nonetheless, I was their advocate, making the calls to doctors, pharmacy, respiratory, lab and others, and even their family to ensure everything possible was taking place to improve their condition. That's a lot of different personalities including coworkers to deal with in 12 hours.

A twelve-hour shift usually isn't just twelve hours it turns into sometimes sixteen hours away from my family. After twelve or more hours of exhausting work, I come home to resume my family life. The long hours away from children and family sometimes leads to broken relationships. Disconnecting from those lives that were entrusted to you the previous twelve hours isn't always easy. You struggle with thoughts of leaving things undone or just not doing enough. I know I didn't get lunch, I had one potty break, so what else did I miss? Maybe my lunch is still sitting in the microwave at work! Over time you learn to control your emotions and focus on prioritizing your energy output.

There are usually at least two different nurse cliques in every department. I avoided cliques, I prefer being my person, besides it can be a lot of work. I find it easier to simply be a great team player to everyone and even that doesn't mean things will be any different. I had proven to myself time and time again that seeking approval from people that think they are better than you is fruitless. After what I went through in nursing school, I'm so done! Now is the time to bring your work skills and ethics to the table and do not unexpected.

I have had co-workers plot against me with other nurses, patient families, and doctors. They would set fires then sit back smiling and waiting for you to burn! It's amazing, integrity is everything. Once you have been beaten, you know what it feels like and you never want anyone else to feel that way. You strive to maintain a reputation of honesty and integrity because more often than not it will be your only salvation.

Inciting fear and intimidation is a big part of our history. It's been around for generations and is no more than bullying. At least that's what we call it when it happens in the schools; There's a campaign that protects kids. When it happens in the workplace among professionals it is looked at differently. You file a complaint and you become the problem and you are faced with excuses for the behavior. " they didn't mean it like that ", "you know how he is", "he's always been like that ", or "you are being too sensitive". Or if there's a reprimand, suddenly you become a troublemaker giving everyone permission to exclude or alienate you. This type of behavior is meant to break your spirit. Somehow people get comfortable with that rather than doing the right thing. With prayer and Isaiah 54:17, I'm still standing. You can't change people, but you can change the way they make you feel.

Overcoming fear and intimidation is essential to success. The mindset seems to be that I am bigger and stronger, and a good worker and the other nurse is not as strong, so assignments are based on some plantation mentality. However, my philosophy is equal work for equal pay. The moment arrives, I could feel the disdain in the air, I am given this horrific assignment. One co-worker suggested it may be a little heavy, but I could let her know if I needed help. Others made excuses because they shouldn't change my assignment. I remained focused because I refused to act out, get loud, hostile, or walk out. After the report, I slip away to the nearest bathroom choking to hold back the tears. I returned to the work area, it was as if they had gotten together and decided to put me under a quiet watchful eye, distancing themselves politely, waiting for a fallout.

I went about my usual tasks thinking, I've been here before and I can rise above this again. That day I took advantage of every opportunity to smile and let them know I was okay with my assignment. It wasn't the first horrific assignment or the last, but they knew that they would have to put in some extra effort to top that one. It's difficult most times to surround yourself with positivity but avoid allowing negativity to consume you. It's never going to be over, and the work is never done.

I have to ask, how is it that nurses you work beside every day don't notice the most obvious and blatant forms of injustice. They seem to have time to go home after work and bring in baked goods the following day. Several nurses can have a social hour at the desk in the middle of a busy shift. They are wondering where I am and why I haven't come to get some brownies. When I get home from work, there's no baking, I succumb to exhaustion. When they are having social hour I'm up to my elbows in a difficult task. Lastly, they weren't even looking for me and NO, I don't want your brownies! What was meant to break me, made me stronger. I smiled victoriously, knowing it's not over yet! There's always that light that shines so bright even in my darkest moments.

Working in a military hospital though was quite different maybe because of the rapid turnovers of active-duty nursing personnel. The environment was rather high-strung but very diverse. Most dilemmas were usually due to power struggles between the ranks. The two words most familiar and memorable were conserve and improvise. There was more autonomy in this organization, and I felt that they valued training and skills. I was able to surpass previous skill boundaries, functioning above and beyond what I thought was my limit. I floated between ICU and the ED, especially on nights during mass casualty exercises. The ICU frequently turned into PACU of which I was also cross trained to work.

I was later offered another position in a hospital ICU/CCU. I would be the first LPN to ever work in this unit, based on past experiences I was skeptical. The head nurse was genuinely excited about the possibility. She advocated for my acceptance and training, helping me maintain my ACLS certification, and included me in training for every task that was within my scope under her supervision. There was some resentment and speculation at first but as I grew and became a bonafide member of the team, this was one of the most rewarding experiences in my career. I was always eager to learn and to help others. One of my favorite co-workers and my outstanding mentor was having a very difficult time with a very difficult patient. She had become very frustrated almost to tears as she stormed across the unit with her arms full of linens and supplies. This was disturbing and I could not go to lunch and leave her without any help. I went in, not taking no for an answer, insisting on helping her. It was one of those situations where you had to laugh to keep from crying. We searched for IV sites together, bathe the patient, changed linens, and tidied the room. When we worked together, we were a team, and we would always bring laughter. Her patient was intubated, and it was all we could do to keep our composure. Maybe it was exhaustion or hunger, Nonetheless, we had developed a chemistry that was rare between a white registered nurse and a black practical nurse. I knew she needed help and I gave up my lunch to be there for her. She was her own hero but just having me there made the difference. The stress levels can be high and overwhelming and so it is not unusual to find yourself sacrificing your time to take care of others.

Over time, supervisors and nurses from other departments would call upon me to help find veins or draw blood from their patients. I enjoyed helping for a while, then it became too much. Sometimes patients were put through relentless trauma so by the time I would get to them they had no trust; they were frustrated, and I had to call on the Lord. Lots of times it would be, " you only get one stick" I would smile and say, "relax that's all God requires." Divine intervention never fails! Being a part of this critical care unit was a stellar moment in my career, opening the door for other LPNs.

I was proud to be able to move on, I wasn't afraid to give up the position or the co-workers I had become to love as family.

Overcoming Darkness

I transferred my credits to an HBCU as a non-traditional student, meaning I had been out of school for over 10 years, a single parent working two jobs with three children. I graduated with a BS degree, in a double major with a teaching track. I would frequently be the minority in most of my classes which were sort of strange at that particular time but has since become a norm. My morning math professor was white American. He started the class off every morning proclaiming his power over the syllabus followed by reminders of drop/add deadlines. Students were chuckling with him, but not me, I was serious about my time and money and it was as if my pending withdrawal or failure was being entertained. The negativity was a distraction and I felt defeated, I found myself withdrawing from that class. I resumed that class the following semester with an Asian American professor who was highly recommended by my peers. I got the support and extra class time I needed to pass math. The fact that I passed Analytical math with a B+, made me feel so proud and accomplished. That was my light!

My evening professors, one African and the other Native American were like an answer to a prayer. They were able to connect with me. When I had childcare issues, they each were very supportive, even allowing my six-year-old daughter to sit in class with me on occasion. When I needed extra help, they made time to advise me and provided me with the necessary resources. With much gratitude, I still applaud their dedication to student success and their philosophies: "student success enriches communities" and " if you don't put nothing in, you can't get nothing out." The following year the university's student government was able to gain attention to the alarming failure ratio of black and brown people in the professor's math class. Finally, a barrier was removed and there was a glimmer of hope for students of all ethnic backgrounds.

In Pursuit of Light

I continued to work in nursing part-time while completing my student teaching. At graduation, I received the most promising health educator award from my department at the University. I was offered a job teaching health occupations education in a local high school. From there I was recruited for a job out of state to implement a high school health education program in an impoverished community. I took the job for several reasons, one curiosity, two a new challenge, and thirdly because It would pay off the balance of my student loans in three years. The move was difficult, the pay wasn't great, but I stuck it out. While there I worked weekends in a Level one trauma center ED to supplement my income. After my three years were up. I applied for other positions at the hospital and was appointed as a regional community health educator for chronic disease. The hospital foundation was supportive, and I was able to co-produce health education segments such as hypertension in African American males on a local tv station.

In the meantime, my mom's health had begun to decline and the need to relocate became a priority. The hospital regretted my leaving and the ED staff held a per diem slot for me so I could come back and work whenever I wanted to. I did take advantage of the offer and would take the hour and a half drive occasionally because I missed the job and the people. It was through this experience that I gained an interest in travel nursing. I became my mom's primary caregiver alongside her husband who was also struggling with multiple co-morbidities. I was working 12-hour shifts, spending many nights in her hospital room, and returning to work for another shift. This went on for months, literally living out of my car.

Travel nursing is very difficult, meaning the assignment can be tailored to make you wish you had stayed home. All skill competencies are completed online. You show up. You are given an assignment with minimal orientation or no orientation. Hospitals are not all the same especially when it comes to technology. Usually, the most difficult part is acclamation to the computer system. Next is finding a place to store your personal belongings and finding a bathroom. The one thing that never changes is the patients. You need to establish a routine and stick to your standards. You will find a lot of things being carried out differently. However, there's also an opportunity to learn new and innovative ways of doing things. Your shift is usually predominantly travelers, and everyone is trying to find their way. You are just the travel nurse. No one remembers your name, and no one cares. You are the one still there from your shift after everyone else goes home.

I've had staff ask my name and in the same breath ask for donations for a baby shower, birthday, or farewell dinner. Other times they are socializing in the break room and you're the only one on the floor. Most of the time you feel invisible. Sometimes it's a good thing and to your advantage. Other times you need help and no one to be found. I've never liked being around long enough to get sucked into the politics. Believe me, it can happen and can happen unknowingly.

Working during the Pandemic

I was completing an assignment in Manhattan when the Coronavirus pandemic hit. I did my first pandemic assignment in Boston with the intent of being able to return to my home in Brooklyn every two weeks. I did not know how to prepare for this assignment. With other assignments there was more information, this assignment was vague, and I was requested to report ASAP. Our country and our leadership were in disarray. There were no clear-cut answers to anything regarding the pandemic, all we knew was that thousands of people were dying every day, facilities were running out of beds, and funeral homes were unable to accommodate the death rate. The healthcare system was overwhelmed, and they were willing to accept any healthcare worker, any licensure, for any wage. Nurses and other healthcare workers got attention like never before. We were able to get emergency licensing to work almost anywhere we wanted free of charge. This would include travel and room and board. The entire country all of a sudden had opened up to healthcare workers, allowing diverse and shared experiences. Our strength, dedication, and endurance were put to the test! So many nurses lost their lives fighting for the lives of others because, so little was known in the beginning. So many of us lived in fear at work daily because of the unknown and speculation from the media.

I reported to a facility that had been converted specifically for the care of positive patients. The unit was being predominantly covered by travelers. More than three fourth of the regular employees were out with symptoms or hospitalized or deceased from the virus. The few regular employees were recovering victims of Covid. They were returning to a workspace with a lot of strangers and changes. They returned grieving the loss of co-workers, loss of family members, and their possible involvement in the exposure. The climate at the nursing station was so different from any I have ever seen. The muffled conversations, jumpsuits, masks, and goggles were almost frightening, air machines roaring in the background made eye contact our greatest communication. Alarms from oxygen equipment in inpatient rooms were almost constant. The phones flooded with callers checking on their loved ones because no visits were allowed. The place seemed dark and dreary; we were told to keep all the window blinds closed because family members would lurk around outside looking for their loved ones. It seemed cruel but of course, we had to protect everyone's privacy. There were occasions that family members called, and I would secretly arrange a window visit. Closing the room door allowing the light in, sharing a tearful moment with a family was rejuvenating. I was able to release tears, reclaim my identity and purpose.

For every two that died, four or more new victims would replace them. The turnover was pretty rapid. The experience is what you would expect in a combat zone. I only got to see two patients discharged home during my assignment and choking back tears, which warmed my heart. Finally, Covid testing began for healthcare workers. Every seven days we were having our sinuses traumatized and then wait in fear for three days for the results. We were always short-staffed and if you were positive, you were sent home for 14 days or longer until you had a negative test.

There were days I didn't go to the bathroom or meal breaks because either I was concerned about a patient's oxygen levels or was afraid of exposure or not having safe protective equipment when I went back on the floor. Our days were filled with long hours of hard work sometimes using makeshift equipment and supplies. I can remember wearing trash bags that were donated by a community organization that had cut openings for our heads and arms. I can remember that being all we had and wearing them all day drenched with perspiration. I remember going home at the end of shift feeling filthy and defeated. It wasn't because I didn't do my best but because it was like working in a third-world environment because supplies were held up or being stockpiled by bureaucrats. Along with the extreme levels of stress, mixed levels of anxiety, and depression, the pandemic was real!

Today I can only remember numbness and that's how I sum it up. The entire experience was numbing. Most of the time, I would simply go to my room shower, and lay in n a stupor for hours. I would go back to Brooklyn for the weekend and pretty much do the same, driving 3 1/2 hours with only a vague remembrance of the trip. What healthcare workers face is universal. What nurses face is sometimes unbelievable. Nursing will never just be about clocking in and out, passing medications, signing charts, and going home. You are touching lives and lives are touching you. You are making a difference, changing perspectives, and giving hope to those that have been traumatized from past healthcare experiences.

Nursing is one of those professions where you don't buy things with money but with hours on your life. Invest in yourself. Learn meditation and relaxation. Avoid sugary snacks that keep you on a roller coaster. Use your energy to turn negativity into positive outcomes. Make time for family, charity begins at home and there's someone in every family that needs our knowledge and skills. My Aunt Ella Mae calls me "the family doctor." She trusts me as a second opinion and sometimes needs help with making health care decisions. I don't always have answers, but I always know someone who does. I always applaud them for asking questions and seeking more information about her health conditions. This is something that I strongly advocate for everyone. I'm dedicating my story to her for all the love and faith she has entrusted in me. She is my hero!

Yes, I have made some mistakes along the way, had some heartbreaks and lots of losses but through it all, I'm still standing. Nursing has made me more aware of who I am and how I want to be perceived. I declare that my legacy will embody fearlessness, perseverance, and the willingness to do the right thing. I am resilient and I am a black nurse.

Aron King

Aron King

MSN, RN

Originally from San Diego, Aron moved to Sacramento with his family in 2000 and attended Encina High School. His interest in science led him to join the school's health academy where he was first exposed to the nursing profession. Leaving Sacramento to attend nursing school in Northern California, Aron organized the community college's first nursing club. As president of the nursing club, he worked to engage members in community service that was particularly focused on public health.

As a registered nurse, Aron has had the opportunity to work in both cardiac telemetry and medical intensive care units. He currently serves as an Assistant Manager at a Trauma One Medical Center in Northern California. Aron has gone on to receive his Bachelor of Science in Nursing from the University of Texas, Arlington and Master of Science from University of California, Davis. His graduate research focus was on **prevalence of microaggressions and the impact on satisfaction and symptoms of depression in graduate nursing students of color.** Aron is the Secretary for Capitol City Black Nurses Association, a local chapter of the National Black Nurses Association. As a nurse leader, his goal is to increase diversity in the nursing workforce through outreach particularly in Hispanic and African American communities.

Overcoming Obstacles

I always ask a lot of questions. It is something that I constantly did as a child that has carried over well into my career as a nurse. In addition to being a quick way of assessing a patient's neuro functions, it helps you to build rapport. Often, I find myself sitting in a patient's room and just chatting. It interests me to find out where people come from and how it is that they came to be. Where they went to school, what is it that they did for a living, do they have children, how they got to California, and why Sacramento? Nurses on my unit get the same treatment. The quieter they are on the unit, the more interested I am in their story. Everybody has a story about how it is that they came into nursing, but Black nurses often have a more remarkable story to tell.

As you could imagine, I've listened to many stories from Black nurses on my units. I've come to understand that resilience isn't developed in nursing training but is more of an innate ability existing within us. Resiliency often manifested long before we began to even consider nursing as a profession. When looking back at my own story, I don't believe it to be less fortunate than any other child of a single parent. My family and I moved frequently during my childhood and at one time were even close to being homeless. One of my biggest transitions was a move from San Diego, Ca to Oakland, Ca in 1995. Growing up in East Oakland exposed me to many of the issues that plague poor Black neighborhoods. Drug addiction, alcoholism, and violence were just a few of the things that I had never blatantly experienced in San Diego.

I very clearly recall an experience that I had with a teacher in the 5th grade. Just before moving to Eastside, my family and I stayed in a predominately Asian neighborhood in Oakland. Although the school had a fair number of Black students, the majority of my class, including the teacher, was of Asian background. While being one of two Black students in the classroom wasn't a unique experience for me, I had never once encountered a situation where I was singled out in a classroom. I had always been very fond of my teachers as a child but was now in a situation where I was being bullied by one.

I remember the bullying starting after my mom contacted Mrs. M about my poor performance on consecutive exams. She was concerned that my desk being within proximity to the door was distracting me from learning. That was the first of many conversations that my mom had with Mrs. M about possible solutions. "Well, we need to move Aron to a new desk because his mommy doesn't want him sitting by the door," she said at the start of one class. After my mom requested more transparency about my homework grades, Mrs. M taped a paper to my desk which displayed my poor grades for all to see. Even as a 5th grader, I remember the anxiety that I went through every morning as I entered my classroom fearful of what would happen next. "Are you really crying!? Crybaby Aron needs to go stand in the corner so that everybody can see him cry!" she announced one afternoon when I burst into tears after returning from lunch. After the fear, stress, and anxiety became overwhelming, I decided to finally tell my mom.

I often ask myself why I waited so long. It's interesting how victim-blaming even occurs internally. Looking back, I think I may have been considering all the possible outcomes. What if I had to change schools? Our apartment is so close to the school allowed my brother and I to walk home most days. Would we have to move? My mom loved our neighborhood! Our apartment was big, the complex was clean, and the neighborhood was safe. In the end, none of this mattered to my mom. She was concerned about ME. She would later tell me as an adult how disappointed she was in herself because she failed to find this all out earlier on her own. My mom also later described how her boyfriend at the time burst into tears when she told him. "This could break him," he said referring to the long-term psychological trauma that could result from this experience. Looking back, I believe that this experience was ultimately detrimental to my determination for academic achievement.

After a few failed meetings with the school principal, my mom acquired the services of the NAACP, and I was moved to a new classroom. I had a second more notable transition in 2000 when my family relocated to Sacramento, Ca. Although this transition involved moving to a middle-class neighborhood, I quickly found myself confronting the academic challenges from my past. My continued academic failures were something I hid from others for many years. One of my defining moments was enrolling in high school. I had to swallow a lot of pride and admit that my reading and writing skills were well below grade level.

I'll never forget the look of disbelief on my mother's face as she watched me struggle to read a few simple paragraphs during my high school entrance assessment. It was at this moment that I finally found the courage to get help by enrolling in remedial classes to help improve my reading and comprehension. It was so embarrassing but equally necessary for me. I became more active in school activities after joining the Health Academy, a program designed to teach students academic basics about health care professions. The program was recommended to me by a biology instructor who believed that my interest in science could transcend into the medical field. My experience in the Health Academy helped me to discover my resilience and my possible future in nursing.

I continued to challenge myself by taking advanced placement English, Biology, and US Government my senior year of high school. I began to let challenges to my ability to succeed fuel my determination to achieve. I only applied to two universities and was surprisingly accepted to both. Navigating financial aid for college was an overwhelming and complicated mess. Between my mom and I, we were almost equally lost with the whole process. After nearly giving up, I finally sought the guidance of a teacher. I felt embarrassed about the whole situation and wanted to get help from someone I trusted. Ms. A jumped right into action almost immediately after I approached her for help. She made phone calls, helped me complete paperwork, and spoke to counselors at both universities and my high school. Ultimately, I had delayed the process too long and had no time to qualify for financial aid.

Ms. A broke the news to me one day after lunch. She had made arrangements to allow me early dismissal from class so that we had time on her open period to work on my financial aid dilemma. "You'll just have to apply for school loans for your first year of college," she told me. Most people don't think student loans are a big deal, but I was deathly afraid of debt. The only financial advice that I was given at this point in my life was to save my money and not go into debt. Student loans broke one of those rules. My only reasonable option was to go to community college. When I shared this decision with Ms. A, her response was something that I have never forgotten. "If you go to community college Aron, you will NEVER graduate."

Looking back, I understand what she was trying to accomplish. She wanted to push me into the university where she believed I would most likely succeed. At that moment, as a teenager, I interpreted the comment as another challenge. Who was she to tell me that I couldn't do it? If I said I would do it, I would do it. In the fall of 2004, I enrolled in the community college as a pre-nursing major. This decision required me to work a full-time job in the evening while being a full-time student during the day. For a while, I found unique solutions for my transportation problem to and from campus. Others told me it wasn't the best decision but, in the end, it was my decision.

Balancing my schedule was difficult, but I was able to manage it and slip in a few hours every week to volunteer at a local hospital. It wasn't all work all the time though. My high school girlfriend and I were able to get married a few days after I passed my microbiology final.

I don't want to bore you with the semester-to-semester challenges that I faced as a Black male pre-nursing student. Putting gender aside, the further I went in school, the fewer students I saw that looked like me, and the more I experienced microaggressions. I'll touch on the definition later for those that are unfamiliar with the term. Occurring almost daily, microaggressions served as reminders that I was operating outside of the norm for my demographic.

As I began to complete applications, a tiny part of me doubted that I would ever become a nurse. Even after I was accepted into a nursing program 160 miles away, I never stopped believing that I would somehow fail. I didn't share this self-doubt with anyone, not even my wife. Throughout the program, my wife would not only support me financially but also stayed in Sacramento while I moved away to attend the program. We would both rely on credit and a whole lot of it. Books, uniforms, food, drinks, gas, and equipment were all on credit. Not to mention my limited budget required me to move into the school dormitory.

So here I am, a 26-year-old, 6'3, 260lb married man sleeping in a bunk bed and living alongside 17 to 19-year-olds. It was as awful as you might imagine it to be, especially for a student working on a major as intense as nursing. The smell was something I got used to but would always forget to mention when classmates would come over to study. I would describe it as a mixture of hotdog water, diced onions, and dirty earring backs. The dormitory was cleaned five days a week but seemed like it was always dirty. This wasn't the ideal learning environment, but I was thankful. I originally accepted my offer for admission with no idea where I would live and only had a confirmed bed in the dormitory four weeks before the program started.

The town was less than 1% Black and I'm not sure if I was put into that count or not. Surprisingly, my first roommate was a Black international student from Egypt. We got along very well, and he was really excited to finally have a roommate again. He described his short experience with his previous roommate. "He never talked to me much. One day I came back from class and he was gone. I still see him around, but he doesn't talk to me" The previous roommate had moved in with another person in the dormitory. My roommate honestly had no idea why the other guy had moved. With the lack of diversity, I believe it was either because he was Muslim, praying five times a day, or because he was Black. He was such a kind person, and I never had the heart to tell him. My second roommate was an international student from Korea but, he had no such experience with any of his previous roommates.

Stereotype threat is fear minorities have of conforming to a generalized perception of their particular group. I felt like this fear was raging out of control throughout nursing school. My past academic challenges made me feel as if I was still working with a handicap. I pushed myself to study constantly to earn every possible point on assignments, projects, quizzes, and tests. I was my own worst enemy as missed points would make me work harder while good grades would be proof that my efforts were working. Mentally, it was exhausting pushing myself so hard. Emotionally, it was hard being so far from family but, daily conversations with my wife and mom kept me on track. After what seemed like a lifetime, the most unlikely outcome that I could imagine occurred…I actually graduated.

Ask anyone who knows me, and they'll tell you that I have stories and love to share them. I like to entertain friends and family with stories of adventure and humor. When telling stories about nursing school, I always talk about the fun times. I bring up the close friends I made, the cool skills I learned, and the funny situations I sometimes found myself in. Not often do I share experiences that may garner pity. "It was tough" is usually my response when people ask how difficult nursing school was. I don't ever expand on that answer and tell why it was tough for ME.

Dr. Derald Wing Sue, a top scholar in microaggression research, defines microaggressions as subtle intentional, or unintentional discriminatory messages sent through body language, word choice, and behavior. It is a term that I was first introduced to as a graduate student but had experience with for a good part of my life. Although I believe they were often unintentional, microaggressions seemed to occur more frequently in spaces where I was viewed as not belonging. Digging a few years back for a clear example, I recall the first interaction my wife and I had with our neighbor after just purchasing our first home. "Are you the new RENTERS?" he asked. Renters? My wife and I thought that was a strange first question to pose to someone moving into a property publicly listed for sale. "No, we are the new OWNERS." His body language in the response sent the next message. Two young racial minorities purchasing a property was not expected. It didn't fit the script.

My graduate school professor frequently used the term "script" to describe expected behaviors. Stereotyping of individuals based on certain characteristics or demographics. Becoming a nurse doesn't fit the script of a male, let alone a Black male. As a male in healthcare, I was expected to be a doctor. As a Black male, I was expected to be a janitor or some sort of technician. Comments by patients frequently help to remind me of that. Here I am as a Black male in nursing. An intersection of two minority groups in the profession. Literature describes microaggression themes that occur as a result of intersecting identities; I imagine a Venn diagram. "Wow! You're very gentle for a man.", "Oh! You're the NURSE?" and the once unforgettable "You must be an exception to the rule!".

No one was ever surprised when I introduced myself as the valet, hotel bellman, or table busser. I was a simple laborer operating within my expected script. Not to say that I didn't experience microaggressions while working those jobs, but they weren't related to my position or title. It is frequently difficult to describe microaggressions to those operating within their expected script. It was even more difficult to explain why microaggressions were so detrimental. Although I could go into detail with statistics to support the impact of microaggressions, the simple fact is that they negatively influence a person's sense of belonging by signaling rejection.

Physically sitting at the nurse's station, I see no one that looks like me. Do I even belong here? This was the same question I asked myself in nursing school and while attending college in general. This is often what derails students, particularly Black students, from entering and completing nursing school. Let it be said again for the people in the back! "The further I went in school, the less people there were that looked like me and the more frequently I experienced microaggressions." Not only did the physical environment tell me that I shouldn't be here but students, faculty, and staff were sending me messages to validate it.

Looking beyond the challenges of Black nurses, I frequently think about the challenges faced by Black patients. There are plenty of studies that show the inequities in care. "Why don't Black people trust healthcare?" is the question frequently asked but a better question is "Why should Black people trust healthcare?" Most are aware of the historical crimes against black people in the name of science. The Tuskegee Trials and Henrietta Lack to just name a few. Crimes that were done disguised as healthcare for our community. I invite you to look at the current statistics for pregnancy-related mortalities for Black women. With outcomes such as this, how does healthcare regain the trust of the Black community? Could this be the reason why so many in the Black community are hesitant? Why we delay seeking care?

During my time as a bedside nurse, I had countless Black patients express relief with just having me as their nurse. I believe that it's more than my charming smile that wins these patients over so quickly. I think it's the notion that they will finally be seen and heard as a patient in the hospital. As a Black nurse, I can more quickly establish trust with Black patients. It is an almost unspoken trust that is more than skin deep. "I am glad to see a face that looks like mine." is often the first thing I'm told. These moments are why I encourage more people that look like me to enter the nursing profession. These moments are why I continue to remain resilient.

Students work hard before and throughout nursing school. Graduation is followed by a tsunami of stress related to the NCLEX and a rush of anxiety trying to find that first job. After you settle into the perfect job, you work and never really look back. This was the experience of myself and many others. I started to take vacations, ate at more fancy restaurants, bought the yeezys, hit Coachella, and upgraded the house. Why not? I deserved this! I made it! It wasn't all fun and games of course. I did continue to get my BSN and finally landed a job in an ICU. I was content but, was I also complacent?

I understood both the difference that I could make in caring for Black patients and the overwhelming absence of Black nurses at the bedside. I knew what it was like to navigate the pre-nursing journey and climb the nursing school mountain on my own. I had the unwavering support of friends and family, but none were familiar with the path. It's here where I stress the importance of mentorship and how one person led me to connect the dots. I could no longer stand wayside and complain about the lack of Black nurses. I had to move beyond the bedside.

Joining a national organization that had a mission and vision aligning with my own was a pivotal move. Not only did I find community but, I was able to find more purpose in my nursing career. Continuing my education to graduate school helped me to understand how upstream changes can improve outcomes for the Black community. We need representation as nurse researchers, nurse educators, nurse leaders, and nurse practitioners. We need to push our research, push our students, and push these healthcare organizations. As I continue my education and my journey into nursing leadership, I make sure to plant these seeds in the minds of new nurses. We can no longer be viewed as being "the exception to the rule", we have to change it!

Vianna L. Jones

Reverend Vianna L. Jones

RN, BS, MSN, M.Min, PhD
CDR, NC, USN, Retired

Reverend Vianna L. Jones was born and raised in Camden, New Jersey. Upon completing high school, she obtained a full scholarship and attended nursing school at Helene Fuld School of Nursing, at West Jersey Hospital, Northern Division in Camden, New Jersey. After graduation, she entered the United States Navy.

She served 27 years in the Navy as a Nurse Corps Officer and her assignments ranged from clinical care to leadership and management positions, to include a deployment to Operation Desert Shield/Storm, a Fellowship at the Joint Commission on Accreditation of Healthcare Organizations. In addition, while on active duty she obtained her Bachelor's Degree in Healthcare Management and her Master's in Nursing.

Upon completion of her military service in 2000, she worked at the Naval Hospital Camp Lejeune and Cherry Point and is currently employed at the VA in Jacksonville, North Carolina. While working at the VA she completed a Master's and Doctorate in Ministry from Carolina Theological Institute and Seminary, and continues to enhance her educational acumen.

She is the author and co-author of two articles (Ration Organs Using Psychosocial and Lifestyle Criteria and the Journey to Accreditation). She is also the author of a book titled "From Turbulence to Endurance. Confronting, Recognizing, and Overcoming Burnout in the Ministry.

From Turbulence to Triumph

This chapter is born out of the author's journey as a Black nurse. The information within this chapter was abstracted from various observation(s), and personal experiences she endured during her career. In that view, it presents the definition, various factors, and symptoms of being drawn into various webs of destruction which tried to block or prevent her from moving forward in her career to care for God's people. It also proposes how one can break the destructive chains which attempt to prevent one from walking into their full destiny in God.

Black women have been ever-present within the healthcare arena. These women unselfishly worked for long hours caring for individuals who were in need and have worked in some of the harshest environments or conditions to render care to those who were sick and downtrodden. In addition, as a result of their unwavering dedication and perseverance, they have contributed greatly to the growth of our country as a whole.

Rarely have these nurses ever received recognition, accolades, promotions, or respect for their accomplishments. On the contrary, their Caucasian counterparts received credit for their actions and were either promoted or given the financial bonuses which should have been theirs. Instead, many were cast aside, ignored, and not even given a thank you or compliment for their actions, instead of comments such as, "look what we did." Totally taking the credit away from the nurse and giving it to themselves. This treatment has and continues to be ever-present within our healthcare system.

When one takes an in-depth look at these dedicated individuals, they will begin to get a clear picture of the levels of stress (i.e, working long hours with minimal pay; responding to urgent and emergent situations; unequal work distribution or accommodations) with thankless people and uncaring individuals whose wants, and demands are never-ending. How much stress can one continue to endure without breaking down at some point is a mystery, yet these nurses continue to persevere.

To make matters worse, many have been passed over for promotion because of their race or ethnicity, even though they have met or exceeded the expectations and qualifications for the job, especially when they are perceived as being a threat professionally. When they are perceived as a threat, many have had personal and professional barriers placed in their lives and career (i.e., responsibilities/roles taken away and given to others to prevent a pay increase or promotion; threatened to have their licenses removed or fired; downgraded in their performance evaluation or falsely accused of being negligent or delinquent in their practice to name a few).

It gets to the point that the nurse starts to believe that whatever he or she does is never enough to get the respect and opportunities they deserve or desire. In some cases, they feel like giving up and giving in. Furthermore, the skills and talents they have are rarely (if ever) tapped into or utilized because it is feared that they may succeed and outshine their counterparts. It seems to always be a game of competition and oppression within the work environment and leaders have downplayed the nurse's feelings and tell him/her that their feelings are unjustified, and it is only their imagination playing with them. Even though these issues continue to affect these nurses, they continue to be resilient and continue to press forward to render quality care to those whom they serve.

. Black nurses have been taught all their life, that they have to be smarter, work harder than anyone else just to stay within the workforce, regardless of what others may say or do to them to be successful. Our response to those who try to demean, undermine, or try to block us is, "you will never break me, regardless of how hard you try," instead, remind them about what characterizes a Black nurse's success, which is the strength of their mothers. The mothers of these nurses set an exemplary example of what it means to be resilient, endure difficult situations, crisis and survive.

Black nurses, especially those who have been placed in a leadership role have had to rely on these qualities to help them bounce back and continue to move forward. They refuse to be distracted, but instead continue to press forward and transform negative obstacles into positive ones. A key element that makes this even more possible and effective is when the Black nurse is not only resilient, but he or she has a strong prayer life and God is an integral part of his or her life. By having God in your life, you will be able to endure and overcome any and all obstacles (either negative or positive) that present.

All of us are uniquely made for a different purpose and to experience different things. Human nature yearns for the approval of others, and much of that is found within the weaving of comparison. We compare in hopes of being better, in turn making us feel better about ourselves. Comparison is never healthy, nor does it help us progress physically or spiritually. It is a major block that could keep us in a stagnated state and must be done away with so that one can succeed.

When we focus on comparing ourselves with others vice walking in the direction God has given us, we place ourselves in a state of "spiritual and emotional dehydration. In other words, we become so focused on pleasing others that we ignore the right thing to do, instead focus on what someone else thinks, says, or does and act on it whether it is right or wrong, thus creating more stress within their lives. Being driven or led by individuals who have a "bully personality," can only lead to heartache and unnecessary pain. These individuals could care less about you and their only focus is, "me, myself and I," and making themselves look good in the sight of others. So many black nurses fall prey to this, because of their desire and need for acceptance, recognition, and respect and somehow, they feel that this person has the power to do so—in reality, they do not.

My Story

When I reflect on my life and career, I have always had a strong desire to go into the medical field but was not always sure as to which direction I would go. I started as a candy striper at one of the local hospitals to get a sense of what being a nurse was about or could be. I got a great sense of joy and fulfillment at what I was doing and when the opportunity arose in my senior year to enroll in a co-op program (go to nursing school in the morning to become a Licensed Practical Nurse (LPN) and take my regular classes in the afternoon) I quickly enrolled and was accepted into the program. Shortly before graduating from high school and the nursing program, I was accepted into a diploma program to become a registered nurse. A school that I had been told continually that I would never get accepted into because I was not a Caucasian, did not have the "connections" or the grades. Oh, but they were so wrong, by the grace of God, I did get accepted and was the only African American in the class and was only one of two in the school. It was a little difficult at first because I was often isolated and left to fend for myself and find my way.

When you are alone in this environment, there is an inner desire to be a part of the team and not be isolated or alone. Each class started with 48 students, but by the time of graduation, there may be

27 or fewer that graduate. It was a prestigious school, no one had to pay for room, books, tuition, uniform, or meals. Many applied, but few were admitted, so that was exciting, but scary at the same time because I did not feel that I was good enough and had fleeting thoughts that I got in because I was Black and even would overhear conversations as such by some of the seniors, even to the point I got called the "N" word. It took all my power not to react or retaliate when that occurred. I just continued and did not come down to their level of ignorance.

Instead of being independent, got drawn into being a follower of the "bully/popular group" and tried hard to fit in. It would sometimes place me in precarious situations which often got us in trouble and placed us in jeopardy of getting removed from school all because I wanted to "fit in." However, by the end of my second year, this changes, and I began to stand on my own feet and separate from the "bully team" and move forward.

Once you are released from this situation, your focus gets better, and your self-esteem and confidence begin to build. Yes, they may have broken their relationship with me, but I was becoming a better person. It forced me to take a closer look at myself and my life. Even though I separated from the "in crowd" per se, the other group of students who were the "nerdy" ones would not accept me either and I had no other choice but to grow, be independent, and learn how to be resilient. The sad part about it is, I still see too much of this even today with our young black nurses coming into an arena that is unfamiliar for them and they want to be accepted for who they are, but it rarely happens.

Upon graduating from nursing school, the next obstacle that had to be faced was passing the state boards. My classmates would stay up studying in their "groups" and again, I was left isolated and alone. Instead of trying to cram in 3 years of information, I went to the movies to see "Come Back Charleston Blue," prayed, and rested. Several of the students that stayed up all night to study, were the ones who did not pass the exam, which created some anger and animosity against me because I did. Through it all, I continued to work with them, endured some of the sarcasm, and kept moving forward.

As time went by, I decided to go into the Navy because I wanted to travel and thought it would be exciting. Little did I know what I was getting into. Initially, when I went in, I thought it was only going to be for 2 years, instead, it wound up being 27 years. Over the years, I was faced with being alone and a similar situation as when I first went to school. The best part was when I saw myself going into the dependent mode and falling in with the bully crowd, I was able to avoid this situation again.

It was like deja-vu, I began to see some of the same obstacles that I endured while being in school. It seemed like the cycle was never going to end or be broken. The completeness was great; "bully crowd" present, mentoring and support were lacking, and one had no choice but to push forward. One had to learn what they could, endure what you had to, and continue to press forward. Now, don't get me wrong, this did not occur the entire time, there were some wonderful times, kind and caring people who will forever be in my life that helped me get through. However, many of them were not in the nurse corps, but from other corps, such as pilots, ship drivers, and administrators.

Regardless of the difficult times, there were good times being a member of the armed services. It is a life of comradery, learning, and meeting lifetime friends, however, some of the bad times just tend to override the good ones and it makes it difficult to focus and keep going. One has no choice but to become resilient, stay focused, and pray hard. The prayer life becomes even more important.

When deployed to Operation Desert Shield/Storm, that was probably the most frightening time. As a single parent and a deployed individual, you had no idea if or when you would return and what shape you would be in when you returned. The amazing thing about when you are in a crisis, people come together in support of one another regardless of what one's ethnicity, age, or status is. There was an overwhelming amount of support and one's fears would minimize, but never go away because of the unknown.

During the deployment, we endured sirens, scud missiles, constant training, and long work hours in a stressful environment. Even though one endured these things post-traumatic stress (PTSD) can slip up on you without you recognizing the extent that you have. I always knew I had some anxieties and stressors in my life before and after coming into the military, it was not until after I had retired that I became aware of the impact it had in my life. When it happens you primarily in a state of denial and feel like it cannot happen to you—but it does.

When competing for educational or promotional opportunities, there were many challenges. It was interesting that you were told what the requirements were for promotion or going to school to obtain an advanced degree, you met all the requirements, and you were denied when others had gotten into school--no reason given as to why the denial.

Individuals were told that if they had questions, a representative/counselor would sit with them and review their record—that opportunity did not come in my direction. To learn and grow, I began to associate with others (i.e., pilots; submariners; administrators, etc.) who were not nurses that taught me what I needed to do to survive. As a black nurse, I felt like an outcast on many occasions. This continued for the most part throughout my career. Even though I endured negativity and obstacles, God always made a way for me to move forward to the point, I was able to go to school and get my master's degree, in Nursing and be the third nurse corps officer and the only African American to be sent to a prestigious fellowship at the Joint Commission, despite others trying to block or change my orders.

Up until shortly after retirement, I was able to fly on airplanes, ride some elevators (only if they were the glass ones), and go into all types of bathrooms—not now. When you have this, one can hide it so well, that very few people can or will see the effects of the disease. Here you are a healthcare professional, and you cannot get into an elevator or small enclosed rooms. Well, you learn to be creative, and resilient, and try to stay focused on the mission—which is caring for others. This becomes hard to keep under control when others push your buttons by disregarding your experience, avoid treating you as a professional; negating your training, and making you show your training records to prove that you have been educated in this area (even when the individual was informed that this training was done while at the Department of Defense (DOD) and it had been about 7 years since it was completed and I had been recognized at having this training at the current job and had actively involved with various projects as a result of this training) when all your peers had to do is just verbalize it. By the grace of God, the document was found and submitted.

As time went on, the stressors continued, and it became increasingly hard to maintain humility and avoid conflict or confrontation. One of the breaking points was when our son passed away, asking for leave was questioned, but another individual's dog had passed away and the individual's leave was not questioned. By the grace of God, I got through without decompensating or letting the PTSD overcome my character, only the love of God kept me.

As I continue on this journey as a nurse, from 1973 to the present, I have endured many obstacles, been overlooked, had jobs downsized to prevent financial incentives, isolated, and ignored, God always made a way for me to be victorious. So, I say to those who tried to block me or cast me aside—thank you. For it made a way for victory every time

Remember ye, not the former things, neither consider the things of old. Behold, I will do a new thing; now it shall spring forth; shall ye not know it? I will even make a way in the wilderness, and rivers in the desert. (Isaiah 43:18-19)

Kimberly Scott

Kimberly J. Scott

MSN, MBA, RN

K imberly (Kim) Scott is a Nurse Leader from the San Francisco Bay Area. She holds a master's degree in nursing administration and business administration. With over two decades of health care experience, Kim has established herself as a nursing advocate, speaker, coach, motivator, consultant, connector, and now published author. She has a passion for coaching and loves to serve and speak about building community. Kim refers to community as, *Common Unity*.

Over the course of Kim's career, she has experience in emergency nursing, risk management, patient safety, quality, performance improvement, facilitative leadership, equity, diversity, and inclusion (EID), event production, media, and grass root organization. Kim is a past president of the Bay Area Black Nurses Association, Inc. and recently served on the Board of Directors for National Black Nurses Association, (NBNA) Inc.

She is the current chair of the NBNA Collaborative Mentorship Program. Kim has made developing the next generation of Nurses her business. She has been Executive producer of the Florence Stroud Black History Month Nursing Conference Series for the last eight years. This conference addresses increasing diversity of the Nursing workforce and combating health disparity. Past speakers have been Dr. Linda Burnes Bolton, Dr. Beverly Malone, Dr. Alicia C. Georges, Dr. Joy DeGruy, and recently Pastor Sarah Jakes Roberts.

Kim has recently become an independent contractor, consulting in the field of Foster Care. She has worked for Kaiser Permanente, a leading, integrated health care organization in the world for twenty-five years.

Kim's current role is Service Unit Manager in the department of Chronic Conditions Management in Oakland, California. She started her journey at Kaiser as a volunteer. Kim's proudest role is mother of her daughter, Sydney an inspiring young lady.

Kim J. Scott, MSN, MBA, RN
Contact: kim@kimjscott.com
Instagram: @kim_j_scott
Facebook: https://facebook.com/kjscott73
LinkedIn: Kim J Scott

His Grace Is Sufficient

The Early Years

The door slammed shut to the motel room. Just prior, my mom hurled a can of Shasta soda at my dad's car. This was the aftermath, of one of many episodes when my mom would gather my sister, Tetra and I to leave my dad after yet, another marital indiscretion." Get out of here; Leave us alone John!" my mom yelled. She was so fueled with anger, and understandably. Dad was bold in his discretions. In this episode, mom had prepared a Sunday spread. It was a beautiful, but hot and humid day in Jacksonville, Tx., the year was 1977. Dad took my siblings and I out to the park while mom was cooking. Little that we knew, he went by his lady "friend's" house to pick her and her children up to join us. I remember having a great time, I was about four years old.

After playing at the park, dad had the audacity to bring his lady "friend" and her kids back to the house where my mom had been anticipating our return to have Sunday dinner. To her surprise, she was greeted by another woman and her kids. What was my dad thinking? I don't know, but he had to have anticipated a conflict. Mom went off! She started shouting and shortly thereafter dad was out the front door to take his "friend" back home. My siblings and I knew it was about to go down! This was a common type of occurrence I experienced in the first 10 years of my life. My mother and father were no match in heaven, and that contributed to a history of trauma in my childhood.

My original, nuclear family consisted of my father, mother, and three older siblings, Sabrina, John Jr. (John-John), and Tetra. When my mom and dad met, he had my older sister, Sabrina, and brother John-John from a previous marriage, and my mother had my sister Tetra. Their union resulted in me being born. When my mom and dad got into it, she would take my sister, Tetra, and I with her whenever she had enough of the drama created by her and my dad's incompatibility or his disregard for their wedding vowels. My mom and dad had vicious physical fights, using weapons kind of fights. It was horrifying to witness. Mom was no Punk, she held her own. If I were to reflect and think about what I learned from that experience, mom demonstrated strength and showed me, no matter who your opponent is, you better give it your all, and that no man will put his hands on you and get away with it. She fought back. I partially contribute the confidence and strength I possess to her.

Another six years of this kind of domestic violence went on and heightened when we moved back to California in 1978. We settled in Oakland. At the age of ten, mom had finally had enough. She packed all she could fit in the car and left for good with Tetra and me. Sabrina had one more year of high school left at Castlemont, so she stayed with dad. John-John had run away from home several times and ended up in the juvenile detention system at the time. John-John is 56 years old now and remains in the system. This breaks my heart.

Mom, Tetra, and I went to live with her older sister, Aunt Mary in Milpitas, CA. Her husband also happened to be my dad's oldest brother, Uncle Dan. My dad's side of the family struggled with alcoholism. Uncle Dan struggled with alcoholism, as did my dad. Aunt Mary and Uncle Dan had a similar type of relationship to mom and dad's, lots of physical fighting and drunken hazardous events. Aunt Mary and Uncle Dan had a total of three sons, two of whom lived in the house consistently, Ronald and Donald, (aka Ducky) may he rest in peace. We moved from our home in the Oakland hills to live in a room, where we all slept in one bed for a while. Living here was quite fun most of the time, I learned so much from my big boy cousins who taught me how to fight and defend myself. They would bet their friend's that their little cousin, Kimmy could beat them up. This is hilarious, as I reflect.

Uncle Dan was brilliant and was a family man. I remember him driving his green Ford Pinto down the freeway well above the speed limit inebriated. Several times my cousin, Nicole, and I would be his passengers. We were petrified; we had sense enough to put on our seat belts, even though it wasn't law to use them at the time. Uncle Dan would create commotion during the wee hours of the night. I remember evacuating the house a few times. Uncle Dan was creative. Before the microwaveable popcorn was invented, he put a plate of popcorn kernels in the microwave to see what would happen. Well, the door exploded open and the hot kernels landing on the linoleum floor almost catching on fire, certainly leaving burn marks. I can still remember how startled we all were.

Living in households where there was alcohol, cigarette smoking, cussing, physical and verbal abuse was the norm, however, I also experienced a lot of love. My paternal grandmother was a Saint in my eyes, Mrs. Essie Bell Scott was the epitome of hard work, hard love, and all-around good stuff. I spent most weekends with her after we moved in with Aunt Mary and Uncle Dan. She too struggled with alcoholism. Grandma and my grandpa fought too; not so much physical, but volatile indeed. She usually got things going. I remember her behavior changing with each trip to the garage. Nevertheless, Grandma was another example of a woman with strength and taught me to work ethic and benevolence for all. She was so kind and generous. It didn't matter who they were; you were from, or anything. She believed service to people was her purpose in life.

What's Your ACE Score

A couple of years ago, I attended my dear friend, event planner extraordinaire, Deana Robert's Women's retreat. I participated in an activity to determine your ACEs score. ACEs stands for, Adverse Childhood Experiences. The California Surgeon General, Dr. Nadine Burke Harris has led an initiative to educate and train teachers and health providers to screen for ACEs. Dr. Harris says, "Childhood trauma increases the risk of 7 out of 10 of the leading causes of death in the United States. In high doses, it affects brain development, the immune system, hormonal systems, and even the way our DNA is read and transcribed." High exposure to trauma triples the risk of heart disease and can decrease life expectancy by twenty years. (burkefoundation.org). The ACEs study was a study conducted by the CDC and Kaiser Permanente between 1995-1997. The individuals in the study were predominantly white, middle-class, educated individuals. The study found that two-thirds of the respondents had at least one ACE. 1 in 6 adults survey for ACE reported at four or more types of ACEs (https://cdc.gov/violenceprevention/aces/fastfact.html).

Dr. Tovi Scruggs- Hussein facilitated the exercise. She had us all take the 10-question survey. Approximately 15 ladies were attending the retreat. Once we tallied up our scores, she had us stand under the numbers 0-10 displayed along the walls in the room. I was the only one standing under the number 8, and one other sister was under the number 9. Most of the ladies were standing under numbers 3 and 4. Dr. Scruggs-Hussein instructed the ladies standing under the 3's and 4's come over to us standing under 8 and 9 and hug us. My eyes immediately welled up with tears. That activity made me realize that I had overcome a great deal of adversity and trauma. I felt sad for a moment, but also felt a great deal of victory pride for not succumbing to what I had experienced in my childhood.

Why Nursing

In the 8th grade, I knew I wanted to be a nurse. I cannot say it was a moment, an event, or a person that inspired me to choose Nursing as a career. I just love helping people and can care for others as if they were my loved ones. In my opinion, this is one of the key qualifications a nurse must possess. I stayed focused, and in my sophomore year of high school, I moved to live with my dad in Corvallis, Oregon. I started volunteering at the local Emergency department. Volunteering solidified my decision to choose Nursing as a career.

I was 15 years old, and mom decided she was going to send me to live with my dad because I had got caught skipping school to hang with my boyfriend. Mom would threaten to send me to Oregon. She knew I didn't want to go to Oregon. I hated it when I would spend the Summers there. I loved being with my dad though. Corvallis, Oregon just wasn't very diverse, and I felt uncomfortable at times when people would stare at me. I would get angry and say, "Why are they staring, haven't they watched TV and seen Black people before? Haven't they seen Michael Jacksons before? He's Black" At the time, I thought moving to live with my dad would be painful. However, it turned out to be the best thing that could have happened to me. At this time, my mom had finally got her place and doing much better. We lived with someone for about four years. I didn't have my own room. Mom worked at Nation's Hamburger Restaurant to support Tetra and I. She did a great job; we never went without the things we needed Living with dad offered me the opportunity to live in an affluent area, have my own room, and things that really matter to developing a positive self-image and esteem as a teen. And, although this was dad's third marriage, I was in a two-parent household and attended a prestigious high school. I attended Crescent Valley High, doesn't that sound rich? Although I was one of maybe 5-6 students out to thousands of students, I did well. My grades were good, and they voted me as prom queen. I knew most people liked me, however never thought they would have made a Black girl, their prom queen. I made history.

Failure isn't Final

One of my early career failures was when I didn't pass the NCLEX, (National Council Licensure Examination). I graduated from the University of San Francisco with my Bachelor of Science in Nursing in Winter 1997. I was blessed enough to find a small group of other minority students who found sanctuary and inclusion amongst one another. I was a transfer student, however, most of the students were traditional students. I attended Laney and Merritt junior college after high school, preparing for nursing school. At the time I was working for the organization I currently work for, as a certified nursing assistant, (CNA). I wasn't nervous about finding an RN job, as I was already positioned to take my next natural step to promote from within. The opportunity was there.

My dear friends and I prepared for the NCLEX together. Shelitha, Esker-D, Connie, and I were all preparing for the NCLEX. Prep course-check, study book with CD ROM- check, group study sessions-check. I would say I was about 60-70% prepared before testing. I recall Connie and I studying at her mother's kitchen table, as she cooked authentic Mexican dishes. The salad with cucumbers, avocado, radish, tomato, and lemon juice got a Sista right, and in the mood to study. Thank you, Senora, Mercedes Corral. Fast forward to test day; I was incredibly nervous. I got through Nursing school, however, tests always made me nervous. I recall many post-test days, discussing with my colleagues what they picked for certain questions, and always feeling like I didn't do well. Much to my dismay, I would do ok; I sure worked myself in a tizzy.

Test day came and went. My test cut off at around 175 questions. During this time, you would get a letter in the mail with your results. If you passed you had a small envelope. If you failed, you had a large envelope explaining your results. I had returned home from New Orleans, attending Mardi Gras for the first time and visiting family. I checked the mail as I returned to the house. Oh man, my envelope was there, and it was big. As I proceeded to open the envelope, I already knew I hadn't passed. I was beyond bummed. Especially, because I had already started working on the floor as an Interim Permittee, (I.P). In the State of California, you can work as a I.P under the supervision of a licensed RN, however, if you don't pass the NCLEX, and receive your license, you cannot continue to work in that capacity. I was demoted back to working as a C.N.A. I was grateful the opportunity was still there to get my job back.

I was embarrassed because everyone knew I was anticipating passing the test and finally achieving my dream to become an RN. My embarrassment fueled my determination to pass on my next try. Out of our group, Shelitha and Esker-D passed on the first try. Connie and I did not. I felt like I was training for the fight of my life and started studying and training for my next testing opportunity. Connie and I teamed up and continued to study consistently. We both passed our next time. What a relief that was.

Dealing with Workplace Issues

During my 23-year nursing career, I have dealt with several difficult situations as a nurse leader and consultant. I have wanted to collect stories from my other colleagues to bring light to the abuse that I and other Black colleagues of mine have experienced. I can remember my first experience as a nurse manager. I realized that the role I was going to take required me to have emotional intelligence.

Emotional intelligence, also known as emotional quotient or EQ is the ability to understand and manage your own emotions in positive ways to relieve stress, communicate effectively, empathize with others, overcome challenges, and defuse conflict (https://helpguide.org). The four attributes are self-management, self-awareness, social awareness, and relationship management. I was going to be replacing a long-term nurse leader who had grown with the program and she was near and dear to the team's hearts. She was a very kind person. I realized that coming on as the manager as a young Black, bald head woman was going to be a big change. I was the Change agent. I realized I had to be strong, confident, and open. During this time my character and intent were questioned because I followed the policies and procedures of the organization. I was invested in my growth and invested in establishing the culture of a thriving team, that I agreed to a session where my team could voice their grievances with me. The Director of Nurse Practice, (DONP) facilitated it. It felt like judgment day. As people voiced their issues, the DONP realized that their grievances were baseless, and told them to cease complaining. An example was getting upset that I would coach staff regarding not adhering to timecard and attendance guidelines. Conducting formal meetings after episodes of blatant insubordination and disrespect toward me was also voiced as an issue. Some individuals voiced their grievances and others wrote them and submitted them anonymously. I gathered the pieces of paper, put them in a manila envelope, and labeled it "Fuel." I was young in my leadership career and have always been open to constructive feedback. I can always be better. I could have crumbled and left; however, I utilized this experience to be better and influence change. It inspired me to push forward. A stance in Maya Angelou's poem, *And Still I Rise* that says, "*You may shoot me with your words, You may cut me with your eyes, You may kill me with your hatefulness, But still, like air, I'll rise.*" I felt humiliated initially, but if I crumbled it would have encouraged others to deter me from my goal to be successful in leading. I had to be resilient after "judgment day.

Why the Challenge

I went from a volunteer to RN with my organization within seven years. I was so excited and nervous to start as a new graduate nurse. The CNAs I worked with were not exactly happy for me. Many of the CNAs I worked with were Black and older than me. Instead of supporting me with patient care, they made it a point to make my day harder by neglecting to help me with my patients. This hurt in a different way. My people were not happy that I invested in furthering my education to become an RN. One CNA was old enough to be my grandmother. I expressed to her that she should be happy for me and that she should be ashamed of herself. No-one handed me my degree, I worked very hard for it. Eventually, most of them came around and apologized, unfortunately not the senior one.

Not the Gladys Knight Type of PIP

During my career, I have been on a Performance Improvement Plan, (PIP) twice. While a PIP is meant to be a tool to help improve performance and development, it felt like a tool to intimidate, demoralize, and destroy. In my experience, it has been used in a punitive way. It erodes psychological safety. I was put on a PIP by one director, the incoming director expressed she didn't know why I would be on a PIP.

Evaluation called out attendance. As a manager, I worked beyond 40 hours consistently and worked during paid time off. which is my benefit, however every time I was "off" I had to do some type of work to keep up. I recall taking my, then seven-year-old daughter, to an appt in behavioral health because she had been acting out at school and with me. I knew it was a symptom of feeling ignored since I had such a demanding role. Can you believe I was on a conference call as I was driving my daughter to the appointment? What a way to show my daughter she was a priority, all to find my efforts to go above and beyond to not be noticed. My director called my attendance out in my PIP. I worked essentially every day, even when I was on paid time off, (PTO).

While on the PIP, I felt, alone, isolated, demoralized, and hopeless. Yes, hopeless for a Christian who has so much faith in God. I was consumed by anguish, anxiety, and grief. One of my best friends, Christine Michel, had to remind me of who I was and all that I had overcome and accomplished to snap me out of my downward spiral. I had an extreme feeling of pending doom and loss during this time. Another dear friend, Tzeli Triantafillou, Neuroscientist reminded me that stress affects the pre-frontal cortex, (PFC) and causes the brain to essentially not function as intended. I felt arrested in my ability to be buoyant when my performance was being questioned. According to Ansell et all., 2012, The loss of PFC gray matter with chronic stress has also been seen in humans. Structural imaging has shown that the number of adverse events a person has been exposed to correlates with smaller PFC gray matter Chronic stress in humans also weakens PFC functional connectivity the executive functions of the highly evolved (PFC), while simultaneously strengthening the primitive emotion. The PFC provides top-down regulation of behavior, thought, and emotion, generating the mental representations needed for flexible, goal-directed behavior. (Directscience.com 4/22/2021)

Take-Home Lesson

Although my journey has brought me through rough and rocky terrain, I continue to be grateful for the good and bad experiences in my professional and personal life. Standing on my faith in Jesus Christ has sustained me through it all. I may have lost my way, and experienced short-term amnesia related to who I am and who's I am in the face of adversity. The seeds that have been planted in me and the seeds I planted for myself have resulted in bearing much fruit. Being a child with an ACE score of 8, and witnessing my parents beat on each other physically and verbally, and still be a successful, strong, Black single mother is the poster child of resilience. My favorite scripture in the Bible is Philippians 4:13-*I can do all things through Christ who strengthens me.* This scripture reminds me that in the natural I am a weakling, however, through Christ's strength, I can do it all. My faith in God causes me to overcome and persevere over the obstacles in my path. When I think I don't have enough, He whispers in my ear and tells me I am enough. If you are feeling low, demoralized, and beaten down by the trials and tribulations of life, remember what my Bishop, Keith L. Clark says, *"You are Alive*-someone was not afforded that gift today. *You are Important*- you occupy a significant space in someone's life, and *You are Changing"*- cut yourself some slack. It may have not gone as you planned, but focus on what you learned, and what you would do differently next time. Don't spend too much time dwelling on the past, nor on things, you cannot change. Colossians 3:2-10 NKV says, "Set your mind on things above, not on things on the earth. For you died, and your life is hidden with Christ in God. When Christ who is our life appears, then you also will appear with Him in glory." Be Well and Be Blessed.

With Gratitude,
Nurse Kim

Finding Your ACE Score

While you were growing up, during your first 18 years of life:

1. Did a parent or other adult in the household **often or very often...**
   Swear at you, insult you, put you down, or humiliate you?
   or
   Act in a way that made you afraid that you might be physically hurt?
   Yes   No   If yes enter 1 _____

2. Did a parent or other adult in the household **often or very often...**
   Push, grab, slap, or throw something at you?
   or
   Ever hit you so hard that you had marks or were injured?
   Yes   No   If yes enter 1 _____

3. Did an adult or person at least 5 years older than you **ever...**
   Touch or fondle you or have you touch their body in a sexual way?
   or
   Attempt or actually have oral, anal, or vaginal intercourse with you?
   Yes   No   If yes enter 1 _____

4. Did you **often or very often** feel that ...
   No one in your family loved you or thought you were important or special?
   or
   Your family didn't look out for each other, feel close to each other, or support each other?
   Yes   No   If yes enter 1 _____

5. Did you **often or very often** feel that ...
   You didn't have enough to eat, had to wear dirty clothes, and had no one to protect you?
   or
   Your parents were too drunk or high to take care of you or take you to the doctor if you needed it?
   Yes   No   If yes enter 1 _____

6. Were your parents **ever** separated or divorced?
   Yes   No   If yes enter 1 _____

7. Was your mother or stepmother:
   Often or very often pushed, grabbed, slapped, or had something thrown at her?
   or
   Sometimes, often, or very often kicked, bitten, hit with a fist, or hit with something hard?
   or
   Ever repeatedly hit at least a few minutes or threatened with a gun or knife?
   Yes   No   If yes enter 1 _____

8. Did you live with anyone who was a problem drinker or alcoholic or who used street drugs?
   Yes   No   If yes enter 1 _____

9. Was a household member depressed or mentally ill, or did a household member attempt suicide?
   Yes   No   If yes enter 1 _____

10. Did a household member go to prison?
    Yes   No   If yes enter 1 _____

Now add up your "Yes" answers: _____ **This is your ACE Score.**

Adapted from: http://www.acestudy.org/Easy-ACE_Score_Calculator.xlt, 09340BA4CB

THE
TRUTH ABOUT ACEs

WHAT ARE THEY?

ACEs are
ADVERSE CHILDHOOD EXPERIENCES

The three types of ACEs include

ABUSE	NEGLECT	HOUSEHOLD DYSFUNCTION	
Physical	Physical	Mental Illness	Incarcerated Relative
Emotional	Emotional	Mother treated violently	Substance Abuse
Sexual		Divorce	

HOW PREVALENT ARE ACEs?

The ACE study* revealed the following estimates:

ABUSE

Physical Abuse	28.3%
Sexual Abuse	20.7%
Emotional Abuse	10.6%

percentage of study participants that experienced a specific ACE

NEGLECT

Emotional Neglect	14.8%
Physical Neglect	9.9%

HOUSEHOLD DYSFUNCTION

Household Substance Abuse	26.9%
Parental Divorce	23.3%
Household Mental Illness	19.4%
Mother Treated Violently	12.7%
Incarcerated Household Member	4.7%

Of 17,000 ACE study participants:

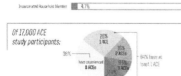

36% have experienced 0 ACEs

64% have at least 1 ACE

WHAT IMPACT DO ACEs HAVE?

As the number of ACEs increases, so does the risk for negative health outcomes

RISK

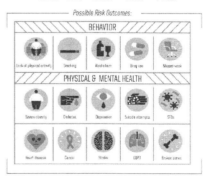

0 ACEs   1 ACE   2 ACEs   3 ACEs   4+ ACEs

Possible Risk Outcomes:

BEHAVIOR

Lack of physical activity	Smoking	Alcoholism	Drug use	Missed work

PHYSICAL & MENTAL HEALTH

Severe obesity	Diabetes	Depression	Suicide attempts	STDs
Heart disease	Cancer	Stroke	COPD	Broken bones

*Source: http://www.cdc.gov/ace/prevalence.htm

131

Panza McNeil

Panza McNeill

BSN, RN

Panza Allen McNeill, Panza is a native of Wilmington, NC, and she has been a Registered Nurse for over 30 years. She graduated from North Carolina Central University. She has traveled all over the world as a Registered Nurse working in various areas of nursing such as Med/Surg, Oncology, ICU, Outpatient Clinic, Case Management, and Public Health.

Panza has currently been a Public Health Nurse for 20 years at the local health department and has been involved in numerous organizations in the community and public health arena. She formerly held the position as the President of the North Carolina Association of Public Health Nursing Administrators (NCAPHNA) and currently is the Chairperson for the Elizabeth Holley Scholarship. She says that Public Health is her love. She finds joy in being able to educate the community, provide preventive nursing care, and addressing community issues head on. This pandemic has shown her that patient education is very important as well as having the trust of your community.

Panza is a proud member of Delta Sigma Theta Sorority, Inc. She has two young adults and one grandson. In her spare time, she enjoys traveling, shopping, eating good food and socializing with her family and friends. She believes it is an honor to share her most memorable nursing experiences and she hopes it will inspire novice Nurses and future Nurses to be diligent when the road gets rough. One of Panza's favorite quotes says, "If you fall off the horse, get back on and ride it out"-Ellen Allen.

Playing the Game
to Get the RN Fame

As a young girl, I always wanted to be a Registered Nurse. From the time I saw my aunt in her starched white uniform to the time the sewing machine needle went through my oldest sister's finger and it turned green because she tried to keep it a secret. I discovered it and tried to secretly doctor on her finger but to no prevail it got worst so we had to tell our parents. These childhood experiences intrigued my dream of becoming a Registered Nurse and prepared me to be the Nurse I am today.

I went to a historically black college university (HBCU). During my senior year at my HBCU, there were some major staffing changes in our nursing department. They hired a completely new Nursing Department. The new Department Head came from a Predominately White Institution that instantly questioned our nursing knowledge. She gave the senior class an exam to test our knowledge- no one passed, not even the smartest person in the class. She continued to give us a series of exams over the year and eventually, the entire class did pass her uniquely designed exams. Her process caused the entire senior class to attend the HBCU an extra year. I remember going to the phone booth, crying, and telling my mom I was going crazy and need to talk to a psychologist. My mom told me to stop all that crying, get back on that horse, and ride it out until it calms down. She said, "you have too many family members to talk to, you don't need a doctor". After that situation, I pulled up my straps and rode out my storm. Thankfully, I passed the North Carolina Licensure Exam, NCLEX, on the first try.

My first employer was the Veteran Administration hospital (VA). I remember some major incidents that helped mold my nursing career while I worked at this particular hospital. I worked at this hospital for a year and a half as a Student Nurse Aid. I asked my Head Nurse could I take off two weeks so I could study for the NCLEX and hopefully return to the VA hospital to work as an RN. She said no. I was astounded. I waited two days and asked her again. She said no again. I asked her what her reason was, and she stated that the floor would be short-staffed. I asked her if she could not sacrifice two weeks so I could take my exam and return to work for her as an RN- She still said no. That night I called my mom to tell her what happened, and she said, "that same horse you need to get back on it and take a different route". I thought about it all night long. The next day, I drafted a letter explaining my situation and stated my request. The next day, I approached my Head Nurse's Manager to explain my situation and requested two weeks off. She immediately denied my request with no explanation. I guess she didn't know that I knew that she and my Head Nurse were good friends, but I already had a Plan C. I had already submitted my letter to the Director of Nursing who was not aware of my situation. She immediately approved my request and stated she looked forward to working with me. A few months later, I passed the NCLEX and return to the VA hospital to work for another 2 years as a Registered Nurse.

Another incident that occurred was when I called a Code Blue, and the other two RNs did not assist me. I had only been working as an RN for 3 months and this was my first Code Blue. They continued to pass their medications with no hesitation. Thank goodness for the 65-year-old CNA, with a bad back and feet, who helped me resuscitate the patient.

Also, I remember a time when I would not release the narcotic keys to the oncoming shift RN whose breath smelled like alcohol.

She became angry and cussed at me, but I still would not give her the narcotic keys. Then, there was also the patient who kept calling me the N-word as I feed him because his arms were deformed, and he was a double amputee. I just thought that this patient needs nourishment and did not take it personally.

Now, my experience at the VA hospital was not all bad. It was a very rewarding experience that gave me some hard life lessons- plus I always said if you can work at the VA hospital then you know the meaning of hard work. I was given the nickname, "Tricksy", from the patients at the VA hospital. They said they gave me that name because I had a quick return on anything they requested. For example, they would ask for their pain medication at least one hour early because that's how long it took the other Nurses to bring their pain medication. As one patient stated, "They are old and slow". Not only did I respond to them quickly, but I also did a spa day on the Saturdays I worked. The spa day consisted of facial wraps with hot towels, facial shavings, trimming off all facial hairs (ears, nose, beards, mustaches, and head), fingernail trimming and foot soaks. As the spa day was taking place, the patients would talk about ole times, family stories and share words of encouragement. We had so much fun- lots of laughter. During those moments, I learned a lot about war, what the veterans tolerated and how the war affected them plus I even learned there was a war tank name "Panzer". I worked at the VA hospital for 2 years then I left for another adventure.

I got married to a military guy and moved to Hawaii. It was a fabulous military assignment/honeymoon that lasted for three years. I worked in the military hospital and a nursing agency because at that time I did not have any children. It was a great assignment. I met a lot of people and formed some long-lasting friendships. This assignment taught me how to work and deal with people of different cultures, military ranks, military lifestyle, and married life. It was a breeze. I can only remember a few incidents that stuck out in my mind- such as the Doctor assuming I was the Unit Clerk and threw a paper at me, then told me to file it. I told him to file it yourself. He asked me to repeat what I said, and I did plus I told him it was rude to throw a paper at someone. He called me a "jerk" and I told him "no thank you and I am an RN".

I also remember the time I worked at a private hospital, through the nursing agency, and the Charge Nurse gave me five patients that were in isolation including a patient on the ventilator. They didn't have to worry about me returning to that particular hospital.

I moved again to several other military bases over 13 years. In my last assignment on a military base, I encountered military personnel who was in charge of the enlisted soldiers even though I was in charge of the entire clinic. In the beginning, we had a tainted work relationship for reasons unknown to me. She tried her hardest to work against me. I had several conversations with her to help mend our fractured work relationship. The most disappointing matter was that she was an African American female. As the saying goes "that was the straw that broke the camel's back" happened at a staff meeting. She was so rude and loud towards me. I said nothing to her during the meeting but afterward, I downloaded all my thoughts, feelings, and anger at her. It scared her so bad she would not come out of her office but at the end of the day, she did apologize for her rude behavior in the staff meeting. After our brief confrontation, we were close friends and she shared with me she had resentment towards African American females with authority due to a traumatic childhood experience.

On the same military base, I had a rewarding experience. As the Director of the military clinic, I was also in charge of health promotion activities on the entire military base. My first year, I planned a big Breast Cancer event, but it was poorly attended, and I was saddened about the results. A few weeks later, a member of the Officer's Wives club contacted me and stated that she attended the event. She was amazed that the attendance was so low. She stated that next year she would support me and get donations for the event. Well, the next year, I had one of the largest events, Breast Cancer Awareness, the military base had. Even after that event, the club helped sponsor and promote any health promotion activity on the base. The clinic was running so well that when I submitted my resignation letter the military base commander offered my kids and me to stay in the basement apartment in her house. She did not want me to resign or leave the area.

Another rewarding experience for me has been as a Public Health Nurse. I worked in OB/GYN case management and met numerous young ladies who were pregnant. They had various issues such as homelessness, substance abuse, poor parenting skills, medical conditions, emotional damage, and other setbacks. We have kept in contact with each other over the past twenty years. The young ladies will stop by to see me, send a message through another coworker, or call me or I may bump into them at a store. When I hear "Ms. Panzaaaa" I know it's one of my former patients. They call me to ask questions about a particular situation or get advice or just to say "hello". It warms my heart and brings a big smile to my face.

Now, I continue to experience small incidents that make my skin crawl from time to time such as when the assumption is made that you are not a Registered Nurse. For example, EMS personnel asked me to sign the release form to transport a patient and the person stated, "You don't have to be an RN". I stated I am a Registered Nurse as I signed my name and discipline in big letters. Or when I am speaking with a patient or family member about a situation, and they asked to speak to the person in charge- "Speaking". These examples helped laid the foundation and influenced me as a Registered Nurse. How? They put me in a position where it was life or death, sink or swim, or fight or flight. Sometimes, you have to know when to just let it be and go on about your business. As my mom would tell me "You have bigger fish to fry". Every comment does not require a response because actions are louder than words sometimes. There are more days when I am thankful that I chose the nursing profession, then, there are other days I ask myself "What else can I do?" or "Can I retire now?".

Nursing is a profession where you have to have a genuine heart, compassion, dedication, and stamina. A Nurse has to have compassion for all people regardless of their race, age, religion, economic status, ethnicity, and gender also including the constant complainers, wimpy patients, constant call bell ringers, and mean/angry patients. One must deal with a variety of personalities daily. Also, being a Nurse, I've learned that if I don't get along with a patient, I will try to assess the situation in-depth and ask myself questions such as why is this patient like this: Am I having a bad day? Is it my race? If it cannot be resolved, then I've asked another Nurse to switch a patient with me and vice versa. This profession is not for the faint-hearted because you have to deal with harsh and unfair patient assignments. If it is tolerable, I will roll with the assignment, but if not, I will gladly ask to be reassigned. I sometimes let things roll off my back because silence also sends a great message.

As an African American Registered Nurse, I feel that we are held to a different standard as if we have to prove ourselves-especially if we attended an HBCU. We have to work extra hard to make a point or make sure everything is correct. Especially when I am asked the question- Are you sure? Despite all the challenges, I would still choose nursing as my profession and select the path that I have traveled. I have grown to tolerate people who are not nice to me as an African American Nurse because my foundation and family support system are strong.

I would like to thank my mother for not holding back on her words and giving me a slap of reality when necessary. She was my biggest cheerleader and always gave me words of wisdom through her old wife's tales. My mother never let me give up during some low moments in my career. Also, thanks to my daddy for not saying much, but when he did, you had better listen. He lived by this motto, "I don't want anyone to be the role model for my girls, I want to be their role model." That's how he lives his life so we could pattern him. He has stood by my side quietly- but firm. A big shout out to my two sisters who listened to me whine, cry and laugh, but most of all they give me their love and support. Thank you to the rest of my family and friends.

Michele Derricott

Michele Derricott

Michele Meeks Derricott RN, was born in Lillie Louisiana, but was raised in Gastonia, North Carolina. She is a proud 1994 graduate of Winston Salem State University with a Bachelor of Arts in Political Science. Upon graduating, she relocated to Norfolk, VA, got married, then began raising a family. She then developed a passion for nursing and decided to pursue it. She is also a proud graduate of Norfolk State University with a Bachelor of Science degree in Nursing.

Over the past 19 years, her specialties ranged from Medical/ Surgical Nursing, Cardiac Step-down, Women's Health, and now behavioral Health. She is a member of North Carolina Nurses Association and the National Black Nurses Association. For two consecutive years, Michele was nominated and received The Excellence in Nursing Award in 2012 and 2013. She has also been recognized for her compassionate and extraordinary nursing care and received a Daisy Award in April 2020.

In her free time, Michele likes to take her own mental health day and enjoys knitting, crafting, traveling and spending time with family. She has also organized and have led peaceful- and socially distanced protests during the pandemic in 2020, in support of justice and equity for her fellow African Americans mistreated due to the color of their skin. Michele is using this platform to inspire nurses of color to advocate for themselves by speaking up and speaking out when they find themselves struggling with racial remarks, stereotypes, and biases.

Michele is dedicating this chapter to her late grandmother Mary Eliza Alderson- who recently passed away. Amongst being a war

Nurse and activist, she was the matriarch of the family who never stopped sharing her wisdom, love and inspiration. Her grandmother instilled in her that she could do anything. Michele implements many of the lessons learned from her grandmother in her daily life.

Black Women in the World of Nursing

Mary Eliza Mahoney (May 7, 1845 - January 4, 1926) was the first African American to study and work as a professionally trained nurse in the United States. In 1879, Mahoney was the first African American to graduate from an American school of nursing. She was a trailblazer, and she paved the way for black nurses today.

When I graduated from Norfolk State University in May 2002, I felt relieved, thrilled and so pleased with myself. To know that you're now technically fully eligible to class yourself as a Registered Nurse was a great feeling. It was a dream come true. I could finally exhale. Completing a second degree accelerated nursing program was one of the hardest things I've ever done. It was thirteen months of no sleep, not seeing my family and a non-productive stress cough which didn't go away until the last day of class. To make matters worse I developed a herniated disc during the last semester of the program which landed me on bed rest. I missed 2 full weeks of clinical and got kicked out of the nursing program. By the grace of God, I was able to convince the school board to accept me back into the program and I was able to graduate on time. I felt like I was sitting on top of the world. I got my first job as a staff nurse at a facility in Newport News Virginia on a Med/Surg unit three weeks before I graduated. As a new grad, I was young and eager to learn. Like a sponge, I was soaking up knowledge from the seasoned experienced nurses. I had a burning passion to advocate and educate patients and their loved ones. I worked my ass off and loved every minute of it. Thinking back, it was hard work for nurses that cared about caring for others. We worked long, tireless hours most of the time without a break. But I didn't mind, my goal was to make sure my patients felt safe and felt like they mattered. The nurses that trained me were some of the best, most caring nurses that I have ever met. They took me under their wings and molded me into the caring, empathetic nurse I am today. It was a diverse unit and I never felt like an outcast because I was a black nurse. They embraced me and I felt welcomed, and the color of my skin was never an issue.

In June of 2006, my family and I moved to Stanley North Carolina. I accepted a position as a staff nurse at a facility in Gastonia, North Carolina. I was excited about this position. I knew it was going to be hard work, but I was ready for the challenge. I was on orientation for approximately six weeks. When orientation was complete and I was on my own, I started to notice that I was given the heaviest patient load, and even though I had more patients than the other white nurses on shift that night, I was always assigned the first admission. At first, I took it at face value then I realized the shit continued to happen and that it was intentional. Then I said enough is enough. I grew some balls and asked the charge nurses why. I pulled out my little black book. My little black book is where I keep dates, times, and occurrences. I was able to tell the charge nurse the number of times I have had to take the first admission- as well as the number of times I started with more patients than the white nurses. After I confronted the situation things changed for the better for a short time. Then with each new charge nurse, I had to reiterate my concerns. Even after that certain charge, nurses chose to ignore my concerns until I took it up a chain and reported my concerns to the assistant manager. It was at that time, things started to happen differently. I had to advocate for myself and talk to all the charge nurses to see a slight change and I had to go up the chain of command to see a real change. My coworkers viewed me as a troublemaker, and I felt targeted because I advocated for myself. I got confirmation of my suspicions when I overheard a conversation between two of my coworkers. As a new nurse working in Virginia, I never experienced these things until I began working as a nurse in North Carolina.

One morning after completing a twelve-hour night shift, I grabbed my bag and was headed to the time clock when my manager called me into her office. My manager informed me that a patient that I had the previous day complained that I was the nurse for twelve hours and I only came into their room once during the entire shift. She went further to say, "this is unacceptable, per policy we should be rounding on our patients every hour". I'm thinking to myself, you have got to be kidding me. It is always something and this is further confirmation that I was being targeted. I informed my manager that I spent most of my time yesterday providing care to that patient because for one, the patient was diabetic and required pre-meal insulin, the patient also had a dressing change and was receiving IV fluids at 150ml per hour. With all that being said, the majority of my day was devoted to that patient. I was furious but didn't let my feelings show. I asked my manager if she looked over my documentation. To my surprise, she responded "no". I said, "every time I went into that patient's room and provided care, it was documented in his chart". My manager looked at me like I had two heads and stated, "well I wanted to talk to you first to get your side of the story". I told her, "my side of the story is located in my documentation which is in the patient's chart". I then excused myself and went to clock out. Racism didn't just stop at my co-workers it extended to some of my patients.

Excellence In Nursing Award

Becoming a nurse is one of my life's greatest achievements. I chose nursing because I wanted to do something in my career that is challenging, interesting, and makes a difference in the lives of patients and their families. In the nursing profession, you deal with many aspects of patient care, and I enjoy the variety. As Maya Angelou stated: "As a nurse, we have the opportunity to heal the heart, mind, soul, and body of our patients, their families, and ourselves. They may not remember your name, but they will never forget the way you made them feel".

I'm walking down the hall headed onto the unit to start my shift. A passer-by says, "congratulations", then another says, "congrats". I'm thinking, congrats for what. As I stepped into the conference room there was a huge sign posted congratulating me for being nominated with the Excellence In Nursing Award for the second year in a row. The purpose of the Excellence In Nursing Award is to recognize the outstanding and deserving nurses who participate in the advancement and practice of nursing. I was overwhelmed and very grateful as I stood there unable to hold back the tears. Receiving this award was one of the most humbling experiences of my life. I come to work each day with a work ethic to be and do the best I can. Some days I fall short of that and others I excel. To be honored and recognized for the job I love to do is amazing. I felt so appreciated. I felt like my peers really cared and noticed just how hard I had been working. Even though I overheard a few of them questioning how I got the award two years in a row. I got it because I do my job and I do it well.

NO WORDS NEEDED

As a black nurse, I feel like I have to leave my true self at the door to pacify white nurses. I always have to explain myself because they jump to conclusions about what I mean or what I said or my tone. Right away white nurses are on the defensive and they say I am being aggressive and mean. You have to explain yourself so that you won't be misconstrued, which sometimes gets on my damn nerves, because you just want to say what you mean and mean what you say, without it being taken way out of context and making it more than what it actually is.

My eyes pop open and I say to God, "thank you for blessing me to see another day". As I raise and sit on the side of the bed, I feel discomfort and tightness in my neck and shoulders. I massage my neck for a moment then I think, let me get up so I can shower and prepare myself for a twelve-hour night shift. As my feet hit the floor, I feel discomfort in my back and my left knee. "My neeeck, My back", I'm laughing to myself as I sing this song as I'm getting dressed. Music, all types of music keep me going. It gives me a sense of push and it lifts me through the day no matter how hectic, how unfair the patient load is, or no matter that the patient just called me a black ass fat nigga as soon as I walked onto the unit. I pop on a Lil Jill Scott, Tamela Mann, Kirk Franklin, Mary Mary, you can't tell me that today ain't gone be a good day.

Me: Walking into the conference room for a shift change report. I said, "hello" and took a seat.

Nosey Jane (white nurse): walks over to me and says, "are you ok"?

Me: "I'm fine, why do you ask"?

Nosey Jane: "you just look like something is wrong"

Me: "Oh I'm good, nothing is wrong". This was my response to nosey ass janes questions for years.

Ok STOP, all I did was walk into the room and said hello and it was brought to my attention that by the look on my face that something was wrong. I'm thinking to myself, is it the color of my scrubs? Do I have a booger on my nose? Shit, I'm getting paranoid and started doing a self-check. Do I have two different shoes?

Maybe my shirt is on backward. Hell, you're laughing right now but I've been a nurse for over 19 years and all those things I just named have happened to me before. As I perform my check-up from the feet up, I'm looking tight and right. Hair was done, makeup neutral and nice, nails short clean with a clear coat of polish. Uniform navy blue crispy clean and pressed, Dansko shoes clean and matching. So what the hell, why does nosey Jane have to say to me I look like something is wrong? This right here has happened to me so many times that I lost count. My response when I'm asked that question is pretty much always the same, " I'm good, nothing is wrong". One day I got tired of Jane nurses asking me that question and I decided to address it.

Nosey Jane: "Are you ok"

Me: "Are you ok"

Nosey Jane: With a puzzled look on her face "why are you asking me that"?

Me: "Why are you asking me that, all I did was walk into the room and said hello"?

Nosey Jane: "I didn't mean anything by it, you are not smiling so I just thought something may be wrong"

Me: "when you are not smiling is something wrong with you? When you come to work do people immediately come to you and ask you ``what's wrong"? Have I ever asked you are you ok when you first come into the room for a report? Thinking to myself, (just because I am not grinning like a Cheshire cat does not mean something is wrong with me.

Nosey Jane: "Well now you don't ask me that, Now you twisting my words you know what I meant. I was just making sure you were ok, I'm just concerned".

Me: "jane Doe Nurse, thanks for your concern, I am okay and just because I'm not smiling doesn't mean something is wrong so stop asking me if I'm ok, if I'm not ok I will let you know, or maybe I won't, either way, please stop asking me that when I walk into the room".

This has happened to me time after time until I addressed it. In case you didn't know, Nosey Jane is the white nurse, the concerned nurse with all the questions. I figured out the way to stop the stupid line of questions is to simply address it right away, nip it in the bud as soon as it happens. As a Black nurse, you have to. When things keep happening that you feel are unfair or offensive you have to address them right away and advocate for yourself.

Not Qualified and Not Enough Experience

In 19 years of being a black nurse, I have experienced so many things, some good, some bad. The experience that stands out the most is when my assistant manager told me that I was not qualified and didn't have enough experience to orient and work in another area of nursing that I was interested in. Nothing hurts more than when someone tells you that you are not qualified, and you know you are. She was an assistant manager with an Associate Degree. Hmmm, the last I checked, to work in a management position it is required that you have a BSN. But who am I, I'm just a woman that happens to be a black nurse. At that moment, I was hot as a damn firecracker and ready to come out of my bag but when you are a black nurse you always have to maintain your composure and keep it professional. A friend of mine calls it acting as If which means going along with something even if you feel it's not right or fair. And that's what I did because I don't want to be perceived as "the angry black nurse". I don't want them to say they feel "threatened" when all I'm trying to do is get clarification and advocate for myself. Things often get flipped and turned upside down and they call security. Oh yes, I have seen it happen. As a black nurse I have to be mindful of what I say and be mindful of my facial expressions before I speak because of course the look on my face and my choice of words can easily be taken out of context and I will be classified as threatening or hostile. Suppressing my feelings of sadness, anger, and disappointment I walked away because I was getting nowhere with her. Fed up, I scheduled a meeting with the director. This was a waste of time. She of course was appalled by what the assistant manager had said. She offered me the opportunity to work in the other area I wanted to work in. She praised how well the unit is run when I am in charge, she even stated I would be a great leader and said I should consider being an assistant manager someday. Yeah right, whatever. We have had assistant manager positions open, and you have asked several white to apply but failed to ask me or the other black nurse on the unit to apply. She was smiling, laughing, and very chatty, or should I say fake in my opinion. Needless to say, after the meeting I left her office, went to a quiet place, turned on my music, thought about it, prayed about it, I said forget it, I don't even want it. If I got to go through all the hoops and ladders, it's not meant for me. All I wanted to do was get acclimated to the other unit so I could fill in when there was a call out or if they were short-staffed and I had to go through all that. This experience happened over 5 years ago, and it still hurts. Sure, I have gotten over it, but I will never forget it. Now here we are 5 years later, and the leadership team is making it mandatory that all nurses orient to the other unit and no experience or qualifications required. It's amazing how things change.

Nosey Jane Stay in your lane

I'm a black woman, a black nurse, and after being married for 20 years I am now a divorced, black mother of three. My oldest two children have graduated college and are holding down their financial responsibilities thank God. My last born will be a senior this fall and graduate in May 2022.

Nosey Janes are some special. Jane, can you just let me be great. I never get into your business, but you seem to stay in mine. Why is that? Yes, yes, yes, I work two part-time jobs. Every Friday and Sunday at one hospital and every Monday and Saturday at the other. Yes, Jane I work four days a week- and hell, sometimes I work more than that if I'm planning a "Lil trippy trip". This is for some of the white nurses, not all. Oh, and you know who you are.

Here go Jane Nurse Ass: When do you work again?

Me: Tomorrow

Nosey Jane: I don't see how you do it, I couldn't work all those hours

Me: "Well I'm good, you work 3 days so it's just like picking up an extra shift each week no biggy". Don't you pick up an extra shift here and there?

Two Weeks Later

Nosey Jane: "You working your other Job tonight"?

Me: "Yes".

NoseyJane: "Why are you working all those hours, don't you get child support from your son's dad"?

Me: Ok, I'm silent for a moment because I don't want to curse her ass out because she just crossed over into my lane. Come on come on Michele Think fast before you curse this Jane nosey ass out!. "You're married right with 2 boys"?

Nosey Jane: "you Know I'm married, what kind of question is that".

Me: "would you work If you were divorced and your two boys were living with you full time".

Nosey Jane: "Well yea, I work now and I'm married so of course, I would work if I was a single parent with my 2 boys".

Me: " Exactly my point and you would probably pick up an extra shift here and there the same as I do right. Try to put yourself in other people's shoes sometimes and don't be so quick to say what you couldn't or wouldn't do".

Nosey Jane: "I never looked at it that way, I'm sorry, I wasn't trying to offend you, I didn't mean anything by it".

This Happens over and over and I only get this type of question from Jane Doe Nurses. Why is that? Never have I ever had a black nurse say to me she doesn't see how I can work all those hours and does your son's dad pay child support.

Dear Nosey Jane, I am offended, and please don't worry yourself with the why's and how's when it comes to Black Nurses and how we choose to work. Jane, I am a Resilient black Nurse and I come from a long line of warriors and workers- and yes Jane, I'm a black nurse who is built to last. I'm not easily broken. Sure, life is full of challenges, It always has been and always will be for black nurses. We have to remain open, flexible, and always willing to adapt to change- no matter how good or bad it may be.

6 Oclock News

As a black nurse, you have to always be on your P's and Q's. You have to always make sure your T's are crossed and your I's are dotted. Please don't get caught slipping. Don't forget to chart something or make any type of small error if you can help it because if you do, best believe it will be reported via email or someone will report it to upper management in person. I meant what I said, and I said what I meant. I don't care how small the error is, it will be reported, and then upper management will run with it and broadcast it on the 6 o'clock news. When I say the news, I mean it will be mentioned in the staff meetings and the daily shift change report for weeks. It's so embarrassing because all your colleagues know it's you that's being mentioned over and over. On the other hand, the good old can do no wrong, pure, smart, pretty, "oh she would never do something like that" Nosey Jane can make mistakes that are sentinel events (an unanticipated event in a healthcare setting resulting in death or serious physical or psychological injury to a patient or patients) and it's swept under a rug and you never hear about it. And the next thing you know, Jane Doe Nurse is getting promoted to be a manager. Imagine that. I've been there and seen it- and it's sad but true. Yes, we are all human and we all make mistakes but when you're a black nurse, there is little to no room for error.

Guilty until you prove your innocence

It's 2 am and all the patients are sleeping. I let out a huge sigh as I took a sip of hot coffee and began checking my emails. my phone made a loud ding indicating the battery was low. As I looked in my work bag, I noticed I forgot my charger. As I looked around the room, I noticed someone had left their charger plugged in the med room. So, I thought to myself, great I can juice up with this charger.

Once my phone was at 100 percent, I unplugged my phone and left the charger plugged in where I found it. When I returned to work a few days later, nosey Jane came to me and asked me if I had her charger. When I replied no, she indicated that another nurse told her I had taken the charger home. Well, "I just be damned". Now, I'm a damn thief. Nosey Jane said, "It's ok, I have another one". So how do I fix this shit? Well, it's simple, I sent out a mass email to all staff in search of the charger and low and behold another nurse responded (Nosey Jane) and indicated she thought it was her charger and she took it home by mistake. The charger was returned to the owner. So, there you go, just like that. When things come up missing, the black nurse is always the person to blame. While not every black nurse has had experiences like these, they're disappointingly familiar to thousands of us.

What have I learned from all these experiences?

With every negative experience, I have endured it feels like I have been cut- and the wound is deep. In some cases, I feel like the knife is still lodged deep within the wound. Of course, I rise from this pain and I keep moving forward because I have to. I am a Resilient Black Nurse and what doesn't break me makes me a better black nurse. I always protect my mental space and perform at my best physically, psychologically, and emotionally. When I am being treated unfairly, I have learned to always advocate for myself and stand my ground.

To my readers who are non-Black and persons of color, I hope this has offered a perspective of some of the things that Black Nurse's experience. Many of the aggressions I described could have been prevented if my white friends, who are nurses, would simply think before they speak, show empathy, and simply mind their own damn business.

The Diaries of a Resilient Black Nurse
Documentary is coming soon!

brought to you
by
Sankofa Training & Wellness Institute, LLC
www.SankofaTrainingInstitute.com